Diamonds In The Dust

Simple Yet Powerful Strategies
For Rural Women To Transform
Their Life And Business

Gerry Huston

Copyright

Diamonds In The Dust: Simple Yet Powerful Strategies For Rural Women To Transform Their Life And Business
By Gerry Huston
First Edition 2022
Copyright 2022 Gerry Huston
All rights reserved. No part of this publication may be reproduced, stored in a retrieval system, or transmitted in any form or by any means, electronic, mechanical, photocopying, recording or otherwise, without the prior written permission from both the copyright owner and publisher.

Disclaimer
All the information, techniques, skills, and concepts contained within this publication are of the nature of general comment only and are not in any way recommended as individual advice. The intent is to offer a variety of information to provide a wider range of choices now and in the future, recognising that we all have widely diverse circumstances and viewpoints. Should any reader choose to make use of the information contained herein, this is their decision and the author and publishers do not assume any responsibilities whatsoever under any condition or circumstances.

ISBN: 978-0-6456405-0-2

For more information about the author, Gerry Huston, or for additional trainings, speaking engagements, or media inquiries, please visit: www.gerryhuston.com.au

Dedication

I dedicate this book to my family.

To my parents, Jack, and Liz, plus my siblings, Gaye, Sheena, and Mason, thankyou for my foundation. To my hubby, Tim, and our boys, Cascade and Jax, thankyou for the future we are creating.

It's time to celebrate!

Download Your Free Strategy Templates to Transform Your Life and Business.

As a way of saying thank you for purchasing a copy of my book, I'm gifting you a number of free download bonuses that are exclusive to readers of Diamonds In The Dust!

These downloadable bonuses will help you transform your life and business using simple yet powerful strategies!

www.gerryhuston.com.au

Connect with Author Name here at:

www.gerryhuston.com.au

www.ruralmindsetcoach.com

https://www.facebook.com/ruralmindsetcoach

https://www.instagram.com/theruralmindsetcoach/

CONTENTS

Chapter 1
Wild Woman 1

Chapter Two
It All Starts with Drawing in the Dirt 17

Chapter 3
What A Tough Brahman Cow Can Teach You 39

Chapter 4
The Angry Little Rooster 57

Chapter 5
Why Shetland Ponies are the Psychopaths
of the Horse World and What That Means for You! 71

Chapter 6
Your Attitude Determines Your Altitude 87

Chapter 7
Tame the Wild Beast 101

Chapter 8
What If It Could Be Easy? 117

Chapter 9
Teamwork Makes the Dream Work 133

CHAPTER 1

Wild Woman

In this chapter, you'll understand
the foundation of how to
transform. With this simple
switch in thinking, you'll have the
beginning steps
to create the life you want.

There has always been a Wild Woman inside me, just underneath the surface. An inner strength, determination, and drive for something bigger. The Wild Woman inside was ahead of her time! I grew up on a property in Central Queensland, Australia, in a time where children were seen and not heard, where women were in a role to support the men in their lives, and because of this, you didn't go against the grain. Don't get me wrong, it was a great childhood, and I did have some powerful women role models that helped shape and guide me to become the woman I am today.

As a child, this inner strength was not encouraged to shine very often. It was seen as being disobedient, too difficult to handle or too loud. I learnt that being helpful was how I received attention from my family and friends. I remember being told I was worth my weight in gold after cleaning the kitchen at a friend's place while on a sleepover. Because as a kid, I thought I was fat (I grew up in the 90s and everyone who wasn't the size of Kate Moss thought they were overweight), I decided that would have been a LOT of gold!

Very few people got to see the fun, ambitious, outgoing part of me. The Wild Woman would occasionally come to the surface, but I would quickly push her down, out of sight, out of mind.

I felt I had to be a 'good girl', and the Wild Woman was never able to rear her strong, powerful, and sometimes ugly head. As a result, I put up with bad relationships way longer than I should have, allowed people to use me even though it felt terrible, stopped fighting for my dreams and started slowly dying inside.

The Wild Woman inside of me just sat dormant and docile for many years, unsure of her purpose in this lifetime. I always knew there was an inner Wild Woman, an inner strength, a light, that had so many amazing characteristics. However, I was too scared to let her out.

WHAT WOULD PEOPLE THINK?

There were times I needed to draw on the strength of my inner Wild Woman, and I would unleash her. And on that odd occasion, she would break out, break free and help me transform. During these times, I felt more like myself than I'd ever felt before. However, before I knew it, I would push her back down and hide her away because I didn't want to be different. I didn't want to stand out. I didn't want to be the Tall Poppy, resented, criticised, or socially attacked for being different.

Finally, I got to a point where enough was enough. I was exhausted trying to be someone I was not! This book is how I unlocked the Wild Woman from within and gave her permission to shine! This book draws on my experience throughout my life, growing up in outback Australia, becoming a Primary School Teacher and my fertility struggles. To the present day, where I now coach other regional and rural businesswomen to allow their inner strength, inner wisdom and inner Wild Woman to grow and prosper!

This isn't about comparison or Tall Poppy Syndrome that Australians are so good at. This is about you and your journey to living a life you love by being unapologetically yourself.

> "A flower does not think of competing
> with the flower next to it.
> It just blooms."
>
> Zenkei Shibayama

THE TRANSFORMATION FOUNDATION

Although we didn't have any pretty flowers as a kid, we did have crops, and crops were so much better because they were green! Growing up in country Queensland, there wasn't much green grass throughout the year. It was hot and dry most of the time, and when we did have rain, we all celebrated. We were in the middle of nowhere, an eighty-minute drive over dirt roads to the nearest one-horse town, which consisted of a Pub, a School, and a Convenience Store that also hosted the Post Office. Our closest neighbours were a twenty-minute drive from our homestead to their homestead, but that was close for my neighbourhood.

The surrounding properties were rather large, consisting of anywhere from 10,000 to 40,000 acres or more. Because we were in such a 'small' community (meaning the population number was small, not the distance between us), we had to make our own fun. We would regularly have tennis days on the weekend at each other's properties, where everyone would come together, and the adults would play tennis, have a few tinnies (beers in tins), and then break for lunch. While the adults were on the court, us kids would ride bikes, roam the paddocks, make cubby houses out of branches, or play with the neighbours' dogs. Only when the adults were eating lunch were the kids allowed onto the tennis court. It was a highlight of living in the bush and being able to forge close friendships with kids on neighbouring properties. Eventually, as evening came, we'd load up the car and make our way home, reminiscing on all the fun times we had during the day.

On our property, we mainly breed cattle, so there were many cows, calves, and bulls. During the Spring months, all the little babies were born, and so many very cute, gangly little calves would seem to arrive in the paddock daily. The property also had cultivation, which was turned into crops such as wheat, sorghum, forage, or dryland cotton.

The thing I loved about the crops was seeing how weeks after the crop was planted, little green shoots would sprout from the rich black soil. Then a couple of months later, there would be a beautiful established crop of either sorghum, wheat, or dry land cotton.

If there ever was a paddock or spot where the crop failed to grow or even thrive, it was carefully inspected, and a list of variables was looked at to try and determine how the results could be improved for next time. Firstly, looking at the soil and the nutritional content, then continuing through a checklist of conditions that affect plant growth; pests, water, nutrition, environment, time of year, and feral animal control, just to name a few.

This is true for us also. If you're unhappy with your current results in your business or life, then instead of complaining about what's not working, let's look at what you can do to change your results.

Like growing a crop, here are the three areas you need to look at when starting any transformation. These are the foundational steps to transforming any area of your life or business. And because I'm a country girl at heart, here it is explained via my crop analogy.

Seeds: Seeds represent your dreams, goals, and desires.

- Are you planting the seeds of your dreams, your goals, and your desires on a continuous basis? Do you have clear business goals, or are you just going through the motions?

Soil: Soil represents the quality of your Mindset.

- What sort of Mindset are you planting your dreams, goals, and desires into? Do you have a poverty or prosperity mindset? Are you planting the seeds of your dreams into soil that will grow crops or grow weeds?

Water: Water represents the strategies you're using to implement long-term positive change.

- Do you have a toolbox of successful, proven strategies to help you achieve your goals and the results you want for your business, relationships, and life?

Throughout this book, you'll learn how these three areas all work together to create the life and business you desire. To get you started, I want to introduce a very powerful strategy that has the potential to easily transform your thinking to help when embarking on this journey.

Above or Below the Line

Are you a glass-half-full or half-empty kind of person? Do you mainly focus on the negative or the positive?

It's easy to blame, make excuses or even live in denial about what's really going on in your life. Especially when it all gets too hard, and you don't know where to start or who can even help you!

As a child, I felt like my mood was always dictated by external forces, for example, the weather. If we had a good season, then everyone would be in a great mood, and it gave me permission to feel ease, happiness, and joy. However, if there was a drought and no rain in sight, it was depressing, and as a kid, I knew I was supposed to feel sad or even angry. I assumed that because I couldn't control the weather, then I couldn't control my life! This way of thinking also made me believe, as an adult, that my life was out of my control. If I was going to have a good or bad day, it was determined by my external environment. For example, the music that was playing on the radio on the way to work, if I got caught in traffic or if my coffee got cold these were the things determining if my day was going to be positive or negative. I'd always be looking outside of myself as to how I should think or feel.

I WAS GIVING MY POWER AWAY!

I used to say things like:

- You make me so mad (after fighting with someone)
- I can't do that. I'm too old, fat, young etc
- I won't succeed. It's too hard!
- I never seem to get ahead!
- I keep repeating the same mistakes over and over again!

On a regular basis, I would unknowingly give my power away. I'd sit in a 'pity party' for one if things weren't going my way or if I had a fight with a loved one. I would stew on it for days, running the fight over and over and over in my mind. Thinking of things I could of and should have said to get back at the other person. It was a cesspool of hate and self-loathing!

I found I was living most of my life with blame, excuses, and denial. I blamed everyone else for what wasn't working out for me. I made excuses as to why I failed at achieving my goals repeatedly. And I was living in denial of the greatness, the Wild Woman within, that was just underneath the surface, waiting to bubble her way to the top.

If you can relate, or if you've been living in blame, excuses, or denial, I've got a simple thing you can do to move forward: - STOP IT!

I know these are patterns you've been doing since childhood, so it's probably unrealistic to expect that you can STOP IT. However, the following is a great reminder to catch your negative thinking and stop it in its tracks! This is a technique I learnt while studying NLP (Neurolinguistic Programming), and it's a great tool to teach your kids.

I want you to draw a horizontal line in the middle of a piece of paper. Above the line, write the letters one underneath the other, OAR. And below the line, write the letters one underneath the other, BED. You'll also find this in digital form; go to www.gerryhuston.com.au

O

A

R
_____

B

E

D

This is an example of your thinking and will give you a quick tool you can use to flip your thinking from negative to positive quickly.

Below-the-line thinking is where each letter stands for a limiting way of thinking.

B= Blame

E= Excuses

D= Denial

Blame, Excuses and Denial are limiting ways of thinking and give your power to circumstances, people, things, or fear.

Above-the-line thinking is where each letter stands for an empowering way of thinking.

O= Ownership

A= Accountability

R= Responsibility

Above-the-line thinking is where you take your power back and transform your life! You take ownership of what's working in your life and what's not working. Accountability is where you step up and accept the things you can change and release the rest. You also take responsibility for what's really happening, no more head-in-the-sand moments.

Next time you decide to see the glass half empty or have a pity party for one. Reflect and see if you're doing above or below-the-line thinking. Then ask yourself, 'How can I transform my thinking to above-the-line thinking?'

Activity: Wouldn't it be great

Wouldn't it be great...

This phrase is a super simple, super easy technique to use that can potentially have a massive impact on your life. One of the reasons I wrote this book was because I wanted it to be super simple to understand. I wanted either my five-year-old Son or my ninety-five-year-old Grandfather to be able to pick up this book and easily implement the strategies with maximum impact!

'Wouldn't it be great' is a wonderful phrase to use when addressing just about anything in your life. As humans, we have this almost automatic reflex where we will jump to the worst-case scenario, what could go wrong or how we are going to mess up! We use our mindset against ourselves by thinking of the negative instead of the positive! The phrase 'Wouldn't it be great' is a wonderful way to start changing yourself from an automatic negative thinker to an automatic positive thinker!

Try this out for yourself. This is a simple mindset strategy to help you start your transformation (remember, I said I wanted to keep this super simple, easy, and fun)! What I like to do is start my day with this phrase. As soon as I wake up in the morning, I say to myself or aloud, "Wouldn't it be great...." Then I complete the sentence stating precisely what I want.

- Wouldn't it be great if this morning was peaceful and easy?

- Wouldn't it be great if the kids were fully dressed and happy to go to school?
- Wouldn't it be great if all my appointments ran to plan?
- Wouldn't it be great if I get more than enough time to go for my walk?
- Wouldn't it be great if everything worked out perfectly for me today?
- Wouldn't it be great if the cattle did exactly what I want them to do today?
- Wouldn't it be great if my parcels all arrive today?
- Wouldn't it be great if I didn't have to cook dinner tonight and my partner did it without being asked!

Throughout the day, if anything pops up and I can feel myself getting anxious, upset, or worried about it. I use this phrase again, "Wouldn't it be great…." And state exactly what I want. In the past, I would worry unnecessarily, focusing my mindset on what I didn't want, creating a cycle of worry, fear, and doubt. Once I started implementing this strategy, I no longer focused on the negative as much, and began to notice that things would start going well for me.

Have some fun with this phrase, and don't take yourself too seriously. This is one simple strategy to get you started on creating a positive, prosperous mindset!

You Are Light!

When my husband and I decided we wanted to be parents we assumed it would happen quickly (I grew up on a farm and saw all the baby animals being born and thought it wouldn't be that difficult for us). However, it wasn't to be so easy, and we embarked on a five-year infertility journey. We read parenting books, watched documentaries about what to expect, talked to experts, and so much more. We were excited about becoming parents and having the opportunity to share our lives and love. One thing that bought me so much joy and I'll never forget learning about it, is what they call, *The Spark of Life*.

The Spark of Life is something that scientists have only recently uncovered, and it happens when a sperm makes contact with an egg. At the time of contact, a flash of light is produced, indicating that the egg has been successfully fertilised. I love knowing that each one of us started as a flash of light! Even from the very beginning, we were shining brightly!

Don't get me wrong; I'm not a Healthcare Professional; I'm an Educator, Life Coach and Author who helps regional and rural businesswomen who are feeling lost, frustrated, or sick and tired of doing the same thing over and over again and getting the same old negative results!

This book is for people who know they want more! They want to achieve their goals, live their dream lives, have a thriving business, experience deep loving connections, and live in a body they love, but they don't know how to do it or even where to start!

I give you practical tools and strategies to help you move from where you are now to where you want to be. If you need professional medical help from your Doctor, Counsellor, Phycologists or Psychiatrist, please seek that out. In the past, I have used the services of Counsellors and Phycologists and had great success. This book, however, is purely to help you get big results in a simple, easy-to-follow the way, on your road to transformation.

Each of us has been born for an essential and integral reason, and the world is waiting for us to show up. Show up as our authentic, beautiful selves. Show up without the baggage of the past. Show up living entire prosperous abundant lives! You have been born for greatness, but somewhere along the line, you've forgotten just how amazing you truly are! Remember, we all started as a bright flash, and even today, we have that same light within. It may have dimmed over the years and now be a faint, weak, or soft light. But it's still there!

I'm here to tell you that every day is a new opportunity. Just because you've felt stuck, overwhelmed, or failed at things in the past, you don't need to do this in your future! You don't even need to wait until the next day to start! Every breath is a new opportunity for you to step into the person you know you want to become. From feeling like a failure to kicking arse and excelling at everything, you put your mind to!

How do you think elite athletes, award-winning business owners, and top CEOs of International Companies do it all? They don't do it alone, that's for sure! They have a team; they have a support crew, and they have coaches and mentors.

This book will be like your very own little Coach. Your guide to achieving the life and business you really want! Not what you think you should have, not go after the dreams of your partner, your kids, or your friends. This book is for you. Allow your inner Wild Woman to break free and create the business of your dreams while living a life you absolutely love!

IT IS YOUR LIFE, AND YOU MATTER!

CHAPTER 2

It All Starts with Drawing in the Dirt

Have you ever felt unclear on what direction you want to take in your life? This chapter will help you determine where you are now in your life and how to navigate to where you want to be.

It's as simple as drawing in the dirt!

I watched as my dad climbed off his trusty old horse and found an adequate stick from a nearby tree; I knew exactly what was about to happen. He was about to show us how he wanted the day to run. This was a common occurrence that Dad did at the beginning of every muster. Mustering is where you go either by horse or bike and round up a herd of cattle to then walk them to either another paddock or to the cattle yards.

We always mustered on a horse because it was a much calmer way of handling stock and a lot cheaper than fuel for the motorbikes. I had been riding since three years old and even won Best Girl Rider at a horse show when I was four years old (that's my claim to fame anyway)!

Dad finally finds just the right stick for the job. There's a group of six of us (mainly kids with a few adults), all on our horses, waiting to see what's about to take place. I've got a theory about why farming families have lots of children; it's because they can have cheap labour for weekends and school holidays!

Anyway, we all crowd around Dad as he crouches down to start drawing in the dirt. He outlines the boundary of the paddock with the stick, carefully indicating the location of the gates and troughs (troughs are the watering places for the cattle). Some paddocks have the man-made cement troughs where water is pumped to, and others have catchment areas like a dam, creek, or turkey's nest (given this name because they look like a large turkey's nest from a distance), where cattle can drink from.

Dad also highlights landmarks in the paddock. It might have been a big tree, a broken fence, or where we saw that dingo and it's two pups that one-time late last year. All of these landmarks are very important because we then use them as reference points throughout the muster.

Dad would then give the directions as follows:

"Right, you three, Gerry, Mason, and Dave. Follow the cattle pad up the hill and cut through the middle, until you see the big bottletree. Once you get to the bottletree, head straight towards the trough in the corner, picking up anything on your way.

The rest of us will follow this fence down the hill and when we get halfway down, we'll peel off and meet the rest of you where we saw that dingo with the two pups. We'll take everything to the trough and meet you there in forty minutes for smoko. Does everyone understand? Any questions?" He pauses briefly waiting for any questions, then continues.

"Ok, see you in forty minutes and remember to check the suckers, those cows like to hide in the trees."

And off we go. Each person had their assigned instructions, and it all came from the drawing in the dirt that Dad had carefully created. We would follow the path that was assigned to us, turn where we were meant to turn, and along the way, we'd encourage the cattle to move in the direction where we were to meet everyone else.

This all ran smoothly, as Dad had lived here for many years and mustered those paddocks multiple times per year. He knew where the cattle would hide, where the most popular parts of the paddock were, where the sweetest grass grew, and where the most convenient part of the paddock was to bring all the cattle together.

Dad always relied on drawing his plan in the dirt at the beginning of every muster and with every mustering team he worked with. Even now, he'll talk it all out and use a stick to draw the boundary of the paddock, the landmarks, the cattle tracks, and where we're all supposed to meet at the end.

Wouldn't it be great if we all had an instruction manual like this for our own life? If it was as simple as writing out our plan in the dirt with a stick. A clear step-by-step process on how to start successfully, what the actions or milestones would be throughout our lives, and how to achieve the outcome we want each and every time! Wouldn't that be GREAT!

Well, here it is! You're reading this book and it's a step-by-step guide to achieving what you want. It's as easy as 1, 2, 3! All you've got to do is:

1. Have an idea of what it is you want: - the cattle to all meet at the trough.
2. Draw your plan: - get your stick out and draw your plan in the dirt.
3. Follow the instructions: - Follow each of the steps in this book to achieve your dreams.

The Treadmill of Life

This all sounds simple, 'But Gerry,' I hear you say, 'I can't do that, I don't even know where to start!'

You're right, most of us don't know where to start! It feels like we're on the treadmill of life; going, going, going but never really arriving where we want to be. You're juggling so many balls in the air; family, work, running a business, career, social life, friendships, needs of extended family, community pressures, our health, mental wellness, volunteering at our children's School, and keeping in contact with those that we love! The list goes on and on and on!

The struggle is real!

You get to the end of the day, fall on the couch in an absolute heap, with a dull headache, totally exhausted, still feeling like your 'To Do' list is growing by the minute and knowing the day has owned you!

You wake up every morning, get the kids ready for School, feed everyone breakfast (animals included), quickly hang those clothes you've already washed three times and keep forgetting to hang, yell at the kids again because they're not eating quickly enough and you're running out of time. Then, you make sure everyone's wearing the right uniforms for the right day, get yourself dressed, and just have enough time to brush your teeth, slap on a bit of makeup, before you're yelling at kids again to remember school bags, homework, library books, and hats as you all rush to the car in a mix of frustration, urgency, and the dread of running late.

When you start your working day, it doesn't get any better. You feel like you're chasing your tail. Your coffee gets cold before you've even finished it (not to mention this is your third coffee for the day and the two before weren't finished either). The phone is running hot, you've got emails backing up that you should have addressed last week and before you know it, the end of the working day rolls around far too quickly! You'll just have to get the rest done tonight once the kids are asleep.

That's when you become a glorified chauffeur to some very tired and emotional children (they are feeling the effects of holding it together all day at school, much like you've been doing at work). You run them to all the after-school activities, and of course, none of it runs on time or to plan! You're covering so much country just so your kids can have the opportunities you never had, and you know deep down inside, they do love the afternoon activities they are attending (even if they complain about it all the way there).

Now to the dreaded dinner time as you regret not being organised enough that morning to put something in the slow cooker, so you could walk into the house to an amazing aroma of hot cooked food, and just for a moment, feel like Betty Crocker! Instead, it's leftovers from the night before when you just so happened to slap something together. And yes, the kids start complaining about this meal too. Even though last week when you cooked it, it was apparently their favourite. Tonight, however, it's not the right taste, you've added peas, or it looks too brown! Dinner time goes from a bit of a chat about our day, to all out-hostage negotiation with your fussiest child (or the child who has the best debating skills). Don't even get me started on bedtime and the copious number of books, the endless drinks they 'have to have'. Until here we are, slumped on the couch, tired, exhausted, frustrated and feeling like you really haven't achieved anything today, you've been BUSY, but not productive. Your time has been for everyone else. Your kids, your partner, your clients, your work colleagues, your employees, your friends, and the list goes on and on.

You know you want more. More purpose to your life, more passion for everything you do. You know you want to feel less alone, less stuck and blocked. That nagging feeling that your life lacks meaning, is keeping you awake at night. You tell yourself, 'I should be grateful! I have a great life. I have a great partner, great kids, I love hanging out with my friends for a wine.' But you still feel unsatisfied, unhappy, unfulfilled, and alone.

You know you want to do more for your family, be more, give more, but you just don't know how to fit it all in or even what that realistically looks like. After all, you're only one person and yes, you've got a great partner and supportive community, but the responsibility of the day-to-day largely rests on your very capable shoulders!

That's when it all becomes way too hard and you pick up the remote, flick on Netflix, and double-screen while scrolling through Instagram until you're so tired you can't keep your eyes open.

But guess what...the evening doesn't finish there. You take your tired, exhausted body and overstimulated brain off to bed. But as soon as your head hits the pillow...you start thinking. Your mind rushes to all of those things you should have done, would have done, or could have done, if only you had a bit more time, a bit more energy, and a bit more motivation.

You know you want to change, but you just don't know where to start or how to start. It all feels so confusing and overwhelming. I bet all those people who have their 'life together' on Instagram, also have a personal chef, a babysitter, an overly supportive partner, or at least a weekly house cleaner. That feels so far away from where you currently are and it feels so lonely, isolating, and impossible to transform or get what you want.

Well, I'm here to let you know, YOU ARE COMPLETELY NORMAL! If you can resonate with any of what I've shared above, guess what, you're completely normal. This is the experience of so many women just like you! If you've ever wanted more, to do more, to be more, to have more, but then also at the same time, couldn't be bothered, then guess what Sunshine, you are not alone. You are exactly like so many other tired, exhausted, amazingly talented, beautiful women.

This book is to give you permission to break free from the norm and start living the life you want. Yes, I can already hear the "As If Gerry! Tell her she's dreaming!" (A little reference for my Aussie readers from the movie 'The Castle'). But I'm not dreaming, and I'm not making false promises, I'm living proof of this and so are my many clients.

What I'm going to share with you, sounds simple, but isn't always easy. It sounds like common sense and you should already know this stuff. But, unless you've been working with a Mindset Coach, Life Coach, Consultant, or Mentor, then it's no wonder you've never been introduced to this information. This book will be like opening a door into a new way of thinking, a new way of being. Because I love giving practical tools and strategies, you will walk away from reading this book with a step-by-step plan on how to create the life you want.

Activity: Life Audit

Let me reassure you that YOU ARE NOT ALONE! This is the experience of so many women who may experience one or more of the following:

- Have a family
- Don't have a family
- Have a partner
- Are divorcees
- Have kids
- Don't have kids
- Live in town
- Live in a city

- Live on a property
- Are isolated
- Run their own business
- Have staff
- Have a career
- Work for someone else
- Work part-time
- Work full time
- Live in a community
- Have kids at school
- Have extended family
- Have friends
- Like to socialise
- They want to keep themselves fit
- They want to do a hobby
- They breathe!

This is totally normal to feel overwhelmed, and exhausted, and not give the best bits of yourself to you!

It's also normal to get to a point in your life where you feel stuck, blocked, lacking purpose, or don't know what your aspirations are anymore! You feel like what you currently do now is lacking meaning for you and you feel like your life is directionless!

I work with tonnes of women who feel exactly like this each and every day! And the best thing is, it doesn't have to be this way! So, let's get a clear picture of where you are right now by doing your very own Life Audit.

I start by helping my clients understand where they currently are. To find their blockages, their barriers, and their frustrations, then help them to identify the direction they want to go by completing a Life Audit. You'll find this in digital form, go to www.gerryhuston.com.au

If you don't know where you are now, you'll never know where you're going! The Life Audit will give you a map of your strengths, weaknesses, and areas of growth. This simple tool is your very own internal compass, helping you identify and navigate what's important to you and why.

I recommend that people do a Life Audit at least once every six months. Once at the end of each year, around December to wrap up the current year and plan what you're wanting for the upcoming year. Then again in June, halfway through the year, to set a benchmark on how you've progressed thus far and what's been working or not working. Allowing you to make any minor or major changes, tweaks, or completely start again. During the Life Audit, I encourage my clients to celebrate their wins, recognise the amazing achievements they've accomplished and draw out the learnings about themselves, their business, and anything else they've had to experience throughout the year. The best part about this Life Audit is that you also get to plan for the upcoming year ahead, instead of reacting to what life throws at you. What exciting things that you want to do, be or have? What adventures do you want to plan for and arrange or what goals you'll achieve throughout the year ahead? This is so much fun and is a time for celebration, learning, and planning for the future!

Personally, for the last five years, my husband and I have a little tradition that we do at the end of each year. We carve out time in late December, where we organise a special meal or sit somewhere comfortable with a couple of fancy drinks and do our Life Audit together.

We start individually completing the Life Audit. Then together we share the highs, the lows, the celebrations, and the learnings throughout each of the months of that year. We sometimes cry and there's a lot of laughing and lots of insights into each other's experiences. It's a lot of fun and a great way to share your dreams, hopes, and goals with each other.

Now it's your turn to complete your very own Life Audit. Access yours by downloading my Life Audit (visit this website to download your freebie www.gerryhuston.com.au). The first area I get all my clients to focus on is the Life Audit Wheel.

To begin, choose 8 areas of your life to focus on, the list below will help with areas you may choose from:

- Goals
- Relationships
- Family
- Friendships

- Parenting
- Career
- Business
- Self-care
- Soul-care
- Financial
- Money
- Savings
- Travel
- Experiences
- Health
- Physical Health
- Mental Health
- Happiness
- Community Involvement
- Creativity
- Spirituality
- Freedom
- Productivity

Just choose 8 areas that are relevant to you. Either what you're currently experiencing or what you want to be experiencing. For example: - if you're not in an intimate relationship now, but it's something important to you, then that will be one of the Life Audit areas you'll choose. The same may go if you've always wanted to start your own business, but it's not something you have in your life yet. Choose business as a focus area for you.

Write your 8 Life Audit areas below:

1.
2.
3.
4.
5.
6.
7.
8.

Now, I want you to give each of those areas a score out of 10 for how they are currently showing up for you. Remember if we don't have a snapshot of where we are now, we won't know where we're going.

- 10 represents the ABSOLUTE BEST possible results in this area!
- 1 represents the MOST UNDESIRABLE results you could experience in this area.

For example, I've chosen parenting as one of my Life Audit areas to focus on. And, as a parent, I feel like some days I'm an amazing Mum, and some days I'm only just getting by. But I know I'm a great Mum most of the time, and I've got a good relationship with my kids. So, I give myself an 8/10, because

I know there are areas I can always improve on as a parent. However, for Travel, I haven't been anywhere recently and I'm really missing travel and experiencing new and exciting adventures, and I don't have anything booked. So, I'll give myself a 3/10 for travel.

Give each area a score between 1 and 10, however, don't overthink it! You can also double up the numbers, so if you feel like your Physical Health is a 5/10 and your Business now is a 5/10, then, they can both have 5/10.

Record your scores below.

1. /10
2. /10
3. /10
4. /10
5. /10
6. /10
7. /10
8. /10

The most important thing here is to NOT overthink it! Whatever number comes to you first, is usually the right one. You want this activity to be as quick and painless as possible. Remember, this is only a snapshot of where you are right now. It doesn't determine what your future holds, only you have the power to do that!

Once you've given each area a score out of 10 (10 being the ABSOLUE BEST and 1 being the MOST UNDESIRABLE results), you can draw a circle on your page and cut it up into 8 even parts. Now, I used to teach lower primary, so please don't think this has to be exact. Believe me when I'd ask a room of Year One students to draw a circle.... Well, you can imagine the outcome, but with a little imagination, anything can become a circle. So, my point here is, if you're a perfectionist, I'm giving you permission to draw a rough, messy, circle-like shape, just for the purpose of this exercise.

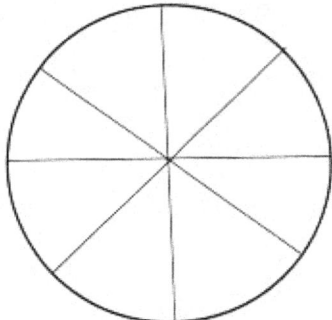

Ok, so you've got your circle and it's split into 8 evenish parts. Now each of those lines from the outside of the circle to the middle, represents a Life Area that you've chosen from above (you should now have 8 Life Areas chosen and scored between 1 and 10). Write the names of each Life Area on the outside of the circle at each line (refer to the 8 you've mentioned above).

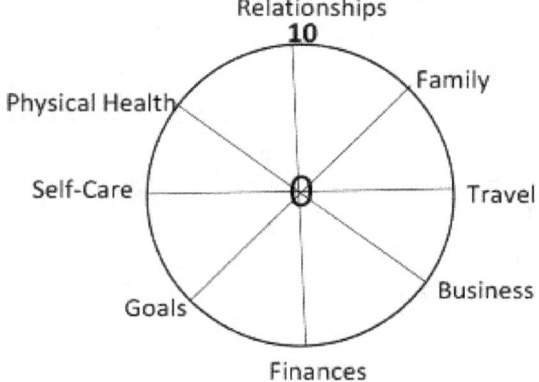

Imagine this is a bicycle wheel and each of those lines are one of the spokes. On the circumference of the wheel (circumference is the outside of the wheel), that's going to be where the 10/10 scores will sit. And as you work your way back down the line towards the centre of the circle, right in the middle of the circle, that will be zero.

Now, each line represents an area of your life, and the line going from the outside of the circle to the centre of the circle is now a number line. 10 on the outside or the circumference of the circle and zero in the middle. I want you to go back to where you numbered each Life Audit area out of 10. And now mark them off on your Audit Wheel with an x. For example, in Parenting I gave myself an 8/10. So, I go to whereabouts I think 8 would sit on that number line between the centre of the circle and the outside and mark it with an x. Then I look at my next area of my life and I put in Travel. Travel was a 3/10, and so, I mark with an x on my Travel line about where I thought 3 would sit. Once I've done this with all my Life Audit areas, I should have a circle that has 8 evenish parts with each line having a Life Audit area written near it and an x representing where my current results are. Now it's your turn to mark your current results on your Audit Wheel with an x.

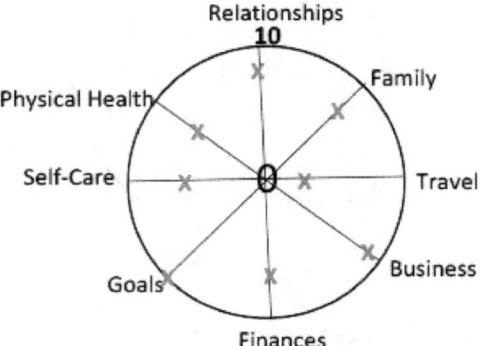

Once that is done, I want you to join the dots up and see what your Life Audit Wheel looks like!

Ask yourself the following questions:

- Is my wheel bumpy?
- Were there any areas that surprised me?
- Was it what I expected?

Most people's wheels will look REALLY bumpy, so don't feel bad if this is you. This just gives you a snapshot of what's working well for you at the moment, and what might need some of your attention.

Answer the questions below to help you gain further clarity from your Life Audit and what you want.

- What area/s of my life are working well for me at the moment?
- What areas do I need to improve?
- What's something I want to achieve?
- Do I have a family or partner goal I want to achieve?
- What experiences do I want to have?
- What milestones do I want to experience in the next 12 months?
- What professional goals do I want to achieve?
- How much money do I want to receive this year?
- What self-care actions am I focusing on this year?

ANNE'S STORY

Let me share with you an example of this I did recently with a client who after doing her Life Audit realised, she was totally ignoring a passion she'd had sitting idle for 20 years!

My client Anne had always been self-sufficient and successful in her life. Until one day, she found herself out of work and unsure what her next step was going to be. She felt fearful about the future and worried as to how she was going to provide for her child, you see Anne is a dedicated and incredible single mother to an energetic lively little boy!

At this stage, Anne's confidence was rock bottom, and her self-esteem was shattered. But worst of all, she was paralysed by fear! That's when Anne and my paths crossed.

Anne reached out to me for help. She knew that something had to change, but she just didn't know where to start. Anne was living in fight-or-flight mode and was reacting to everything around her. She was stuck in a negative mindset and felt blocked, trapped, isolated and destitute.

When I started working with Anne, we did the Life Audit, to gauge where she was at, and what was important to her.

Anne put all the areas on her Audit Wheel that were important to her:

- Family
- Partner

- Finances
- Health
- Purpose
- Community
- Making a Difference
- Business

Anne had never had her own business but had always desperately wanted to turn her passion into her business. Anne was an amazing photographer and had taken so many photos of the Australian landscape, its flora, and fauna, but had done nothing with this incredible art.

Once Anne had completed her Audit Wheel, she realised that Business was a 2/10 and she wanted to start something fresh to dig herself out of the hole she was currently in. Anne had discovered her real passion. Starting a business had been a dream of Anne's for 20 years!

In a matter of a couple of months of working together, Anne had turned her hobby into her business and was now selling her artwork online for the world to see. A dream Anne had for 20 years has now become her reality.

CHAPTER 3

What A Tough Brahman Cow Can Teach You

In this chapter, you will learn what it's like to find your direction and be so unstoppable! By the end of this chapter, you will have confidently identified and written a Big Exciting Goal that you love!

'What can a cow teach me?' I hear you ask, 'What is a Brahman Cow anyway?' It almost sounds like a joke! But if you ever find yourself facing off with a brahman cow, you won't be laughing...trust me!

Brahman is a breed of cattle, they have long floppy ears and big humps, they do well in tropical or dry climates and their calves are just the cutest things you'll ever see, with their big, oversized ears nearly dragging on the ground.

Growing up on a property, I got to be around lots of different breeds of cattle and I got to know each one differently. There were characteristics that different breeds have, and because I'm a bit of a reality TV junkie, I liken it to the reality series called *The Real Housewives*.

The ladies on the show are usually a group of women from cities around America and have been chosen because of their feisty personalities, drama-filled lives, and unexpected antics! Each of the Real Housewives has a tagline that they share at the beginning of the episode, it's their introduction and explains who they are and what the audience might expect from them in the series. They are super cheesy and always a bit spicy! So, I used to do this for the different breeds of cattle that I'd work with, I'd imagine what their tagline would be if they were a Real Housewife of the cattle breed.

Here's what I imagine when I think of the following breeds of cattle as Real Housewives Characters:

- **Angus Cattle** — The Angus breed is sleek looking, it's the cooler breed of the Cattle Industry. Moody, sleek, cool calm collected, can spice up at the drop of a hat. If they were a Real Housewife of the cattle breed, their tagline would be: - 'I'm cool and quick to anger!'

- **Brangus Cattle** - This is a designer breed that combines the best of Angus and the best of the Braford. They look down their nose at the pure breeds and live it up at the cow town disco. Their Real Housewife tagline would be: - 'You might think you're purebred, but because I'm a designer I am the one most people want!'

- **Charolais Cattle** - White, woolly, and look so innocent, but don't be fooled. You don't want to turn your back on this old girl. She's likely to turn and run at you if you're not watching! Be careful of this feisty beast! Her tagline would be: - "I might be cute, but I'm ready to fight at the drop of a hat, just watch me, or don't watch me, I'm coming for you!"

- **Wagyu Cattle** — Wagyu's are seen as the exotic breed of the lot, this lovely lady might not look like your typical Australian beef cattle, but when she's on a plate, her deliciousness will win you over. "I might not look like much in the paddock, but everyone's after my rump!"

- **Brahman** - The hardiest, most down-to-earth breed in the bunch. Fiercely protective of her young, hardy even in the dry and makes the best of a hot situation. "I might look quiet and shy, but I WILL fiercely protect what's mine at all costs!"

Brahman Cattle are some of the hardiest cattle around. They're brilliant for dry climates and their calves are so super cute with their big floppy ears, long gangly legs, and beautiful dark big eyes.

Brahman Cows also have a reputation for being the most protective of their young. They will protect their calf with fierce determination and no regard for their own personal safety. It might be a human, horse, motorbike, or dingo, and that cow will go to blows with its opposition and always come off in the best position.

We once had a mob of brahman cows and calves in the yards and they were all in the far pen, waiting to be moved to the next available pen and then drafted. They were not happy about having been moved from their very comfortable paddock earlier in the day and walked a couple of kilometers to the yards. During this time, the mothers and calves sometimes become separated within the mob, and this causes a lot of commotion. So, while the cattle are waiting in the far pen, the mothers are bellowing out to their calves, much like a mother in a supermarket calling out for her toddler when the toddler decides to run off in another direction!

There was a lot of commotion as each of the cows bellowed to find their calves and the calves cried out to their mummies. However, it didn't take long for most of them to "mother up" (the cows finding their calves), and the calves start having a feed to calm themselves and because they were hungry after that big walk!

On this one particular day, my younger sister Sheena who was thirteen at the time, and myself, fifteen years old, were given the job of bringing the cows and calves up from the back yard. The back yard or far pen was where we'd hold the whole mob of cattle and then we'd have to push a smaller number of those cattle up into the next pen. They would then navigate through the yards until they came to the crush (a small narrow walkway where each beast was single file), they would have one of the following things happen to them; weighed, inoculated, preg-tested, branded, sprayed for flies, or drafted into different mobs.

As Sheena and I went to the back yard, I was already thinking of ways to get up onto the top rail quickly or where the best exits were (as you may have gathered, I'm not the most confident person in the yards with animals that are fifteen times bigger than I am)! I always feared that an angry mother cow would come and charge (run quickly to scare) me. And a lot of the time, in most breeds of cattle, the angry mother would let you know she was upset, but never fully charge at you. That is unless it was a Brahman Cow! Those Brahman cows were notorious for fiercely protecting their young and did not muck around if they were angry, annoyed, or protective. Which is a great thing if you are a Brahman calf, not if you are a human who's disturbed them from their paddock and now trying to draft them. So, Sheena and I started walking down around the outside of the mob to then cut across a section of the mob and move them towards the smaller pen.

As we were making our presence known, the cows just looked at us, unwilling to move. Then we both took multiple steps towards them, gesturing with our hands and voices to move them towards the smaller pen and away from the rest of the mob. We had a group of about twenty head of cattle, comprising both cows and calves. Did I mention these cows weren't that happy about the morning interruption, them being mustered from their paddock, walking to the yards, and then being penned in a small area waiting to be pushed around?

So, we started putting a bit more pressure on them. We started making a little bit of noise to let them know we were serious. Saying things like: - "Let's go now!", "Up we go!" Or my Dad's favourite thing to say when I was little was, "Up you go, you old poo bags!" When you're five years old, you think that's the funniest thing you've ever heard!

Finally, they start to turn away from us and move towards the smaller pen. As Sheena bravely cut across the herd to divide it into two groups, there was a rather nasty-looking Brahman cow, who kept turning and looking at us. Now, you know the ones who are going to be nasty. They are the ones that maintain eye contact, throw their head up, keep sussing you out and avoid turning their tail or back on you. They are the ones we like to call 'feral' or 'waspy'! These are the ones you must always keep your eye on while in the pen. The ones that turn away from you, or move away from you when you approach, have a healthy respect for getting out of your way. The ones that eye you down...that's where you need to be careful. They were likely to charge you, trample you, kick you or just knock you clean over!

So far Sheena had kept her ground and was able to move them up successfully, without leaving any behind. I timidly continued to throw my arms around and call out encouraging phrases to keep this smaller mob moving in the right direction. Then, in a blink of an eye, this very waspy Brahman cow decided that enough was enough! And she had had it with being told what to do! She also felt like we were getting too close to her precious calf, and she decided she was going to do something about it.

That cow turned to be face to face with Sheena, they were looking at each other straight in the eye and IT WAS ON! Sheena, as quick as a whip, knew what was happening and knew that this girl meant business. She wasn't just bluffing, and Sheena knew no amount of noise or throwing her arms threateningly would stop this very determined Brahman cow from getting back to her calf.

The cow lined Sheena up, she stuck her head down and started running towards her with everything she had. Sheena started to backpedal QUICKLY! Suddenly everything slowed down and appeared to be in slow motion, I thought I was about to witness my little sister be charged, trampled, and flattened by a fiercely determined Brahman cow! I, like all good heroes, just froze!

As Sheena was getting her legs mobile, she kept one eye on the cow and the other eye on the fence, making a plan to jump out of the way. Then, something terrible happened! Her shoe connected with a very big, very wet cow poo. And as her foot connected with the wet cow poo, it slipped, and she fell to the ground. At this stage, it looked like Sheena was going to be flattened and me being absolutely NO help at all, just watched in disbelief as my sister was inevitably going to be trampled!

For a split second, both that Brahman cow and my sister Sheena shared the same look of terror and disbelief on their faces! Sheena didn't know what to do, but she knew if that cow was going to continue its trajectory, she was going to be squashed, so she rolled herself into a ball as a protection instinct. That cow was more shocked than Sheena and froze at the sight. Turned. And ran straight to her bellowing calf! This was too close and if that cow hadn't gotten the fright, stopped, and turned, my sister would have been squashed flat like a pancake!

This taught me a valuable lesson! This taught me to be like a Brahman cow. Go after everything I want with fierce determination and even if I hit a speed bump, I persist! I Keep going. The only way I can fail is to give up! So never give up on what it is you want!

What Do You Want?

This is a great place to start when working out what it is you want and how to go after it with everything you've got, just like that old Brahman cow who nearly cleaned up my sister! Below are questions I ask all my Coaching Clients, to help me gain insight into where their mind is around goals and their ability to create the life of their dreams.

So, get a pen and paper out and ask yourself the following questions. Go on then, get a pen and paper, I'll wait for you.

Questions:

- What do you want?
- Do you have any clear goal/s?
- If you have a goal/s, have you written it out in a clearly defined description?
- Do you read and review your goal on a regular basis?
- Have you got your goal written on a piece of paper or on your phone screen and always carry it around with you?

If you answered YES to all the above questions, congratulations, you belong to about 3% of the world's population who have a clear goal, written down in detail and review their goal on a regular basis! This tells me that you're one of the very few people in this world who will most likely achieve huge goals and accomplish amazing things! Congratulations!

If you answered no to any of these questions above (or most of the questions above), then you're in the majority of people. Most of the world's population doesn't have clearly defined goals that they review on a regular basis. This group is full of people who are interested in achieving what they want but not committed to accomplishing their goals. And that's OK. It's OK if you want to keep coasting through life, having wins here and there, letting your outside circumstances dictate to you what YOUR life should be like. So many times, we give our power away to outside forces, by deciding other people's opinions or beliefs are better or more valid than our own.

Most people will unknowingly give their power away to people or things, for example:

- What other people think they should do
- What the community you live in dictates you should be like
- What social media or influences deem is important
- What the news or current events decide are important
- Time spent in the scroll hole on social media
- Spending time with people who put you down or drain your energy
- In a job that they don't love
- In a relationship that's eating away at them
- Repeating patterns that they want to give up, but don't know how

Giving your power away to people or things around you is like sacrificing your life to make others happy. This might sound dramatic, but if you're constantly worried about what other people are thinking about YOU, then whose life are you really living? Are you living a life you love and pursuing your dreams, or constantly giving your energy to everything and everybody else? This also applies to how you spend your time. You might be spending your time watching TV, scrolling through social media, being pulled into a friendship group drama, or gossiping.

Now, remember, this is **common**, it's what most of the world's population currently does. And it's probably what you've been doing, UP UNTIL NOW! I always put in those words, UP UNTIL NOW. Because it's like metaphorically drawing a line in the sand and deciding, from here, you know better, so you're going to do better, and leaving the rest in the past!

When people focus on what they don't want or focus on what other people tell them that they should want, they lose sight of what's important to them, what makes them light up, and what their life's purpose is. I find so many people who are stuck here. They have little to no idea what they want, but a very clear picture of what they don't want. They focus on the negativity, sadness, frustration, and anger in their life and what's not working out for them. Like Bob Proctor would say 'You either have Big Goals or Big Problems'. I know which one I would prefer to have.

When you don't have clear goals, you are giving your life away to what you don't want. We as humans think we have an infinite amount of time and a finite amount of money. However, it's the exact opposite! You can always make more money, but you can never make more time. If you want to see how little time you really have on this planet, watch a documentary about the lifespan of this planet. It has been around for so many millions of years and we are here for such a short amount of time in comparison. However, don't let that get you down, this should be liberating and exciting. This is an opportunity for you to go after what it is you want. Go after it with gusto, enthusiasm, and knowing that you CAN create anything! You are here on this planet at this exact time for a reason, and this book will help you know what your reason, your purpose, and your life, is all about.

When I ask my clients, 'What do you want?' There is a large variety of responses. Some clients will look at me and think it's the most oddest question they've ever heard. Others will give me a huge list of all the things they don't want and very few have an answer for one or two things they do want. Then quickly follow up with reasons why it's impossible to have that item, experience, or thing.

I want you to check in with yourself now and be honest. When was the last time you asked yourself "What do I want?" This is something we don't do enough of. We will fill our minds with things we don't want. Thoughts we don't want, complaints we don't want, frustrations we don't want, feelings we don't really want, or even like feeling.

I'm here to give you permission and let you know; it is ok to want what you want. Because you deserve it! You deserve all the good, the love, the light, the money, and the happiness you want. There is an infinite supply of everything good that you want, and it's your turn to claim it!

An example of this comes from money. There is an infinite supply of money and money is all around us. Most days you are dealing with money, either spending it, receiving it, earning it, or using things that you have bought with money. However, most of us feel like it's scarce, hard to come by, difficult to get or keep and we hardly make enough of it each and every month. However, if I was to say to you that your child or your pet was going to die without having this life-saving operation and all you had to do was find $100,000 within 7 days to have this operation. I know that come hell or high water, you would find that money whether you beg, borrowed or raised it, you would find that $100,000 no worries. I know I would in a heartbeat! You can always make more money, but you can never make more time!

Activity: Writing Your Goal

In the past, I used to feel so worried about answering the question- What do I Want. I didn't know what I wanted! I felt blocked and worried that if I did make a decision, it would be the wrong one! So, I stayed stuck, treading water, sitting on the fence, and not making any decisions in case I got it wrong.

Goal Exercise (see www.gerryhuston.com.au for a digital copy and more instructions):

1. Rule a vertical line down the middle of a piece of paper.
2. Down the right side of the paper, I want you to write down all the results you're currently getting that you're not happy with.
3. On the other side of the line, write down the opposite of the results you're not happy with. Write them in the positive present tense. For example - I hate being in debt. Change that too - I love having surplus money for everything I want!
4. Go through and reframe each of your negative results

and once you've done that, I want you to circle the one that jumps off the page to you the most.

5. Now, that's your goal! Don't overthink this, KISS (Keep It Simple Sexy)!

From here I'll share with you how to write your goal. This is the fun part! In the past, we would have given oxygen to our excuses of why we can't do something or give in to the fear! I want you to NOT worry about the HOW right now. I don't want you to spend any time thinking about how you'll achieve this goal, all I want you to do is write down what it is you want.

Before you write down your goal, I want you to understand there are three different types of goals. There are A Type Goals, B Type Goals, and C Type Goals. A Type Goals are those that you can achieve automatically, without much thought or effort. These goals would include getting dressed, driving a car (if you've been driving for many years), or brushing your teeth. The next type of goal is a B Type Goal, and these goals are goals that you have probably done before, but it's not really stretching you. These goals might be to buy a new car, even though you bought a new car 5 years ago. Or lose weight, even though you probably know how to lose weight and have done so in the past. B Type Goals we don't tend to stick with them for very long because they aren't juicy enough! They don't excite or stretch us up enough! Whereas C Type Goals are EXCITING goals that really light us up. C Type Goals are goals that will have you feeling both excited and nervous at the same time and pushing through the scary parts to achieve it anyway! C Type Goals are your big dreams, your deepest desires, the things you really, really want, however, you've stopped yourself because you've given in to the fear, worry, or doubt that you can achieve them.

So, when writing your goal, make sure you're choosing a C Type Goal, a goal that lights you up and gets you excited! And with that C Type Goal, I want you to stretch it! Yes, that's right, stretch it by making it bigger, grander, and juicier. For example, if it's a money goal, I want you to double the money amount, or even triple the number!

There are a few important key points you need to remember when writing your goal.

1. Always start your goal with the phrase: I'm so happy and grateful now that...
2. Write your goal in the present tense, as if it is happening right now in the present moment.
3. Write it in the positive. Focusing on what you want, not what you don't want.
4. Make it juicy and exciting!!! You should be both scared and excited when writing your goal! You can also use language that's emotion-driven, for example: - greatest love, exceptionally happiness, effortlessly easy, enormous wealth, or unstoppable confidence.

Here are some examples of C Type Goals (for more examples go to www.gerryhuston.com.au):

- I'm so happy and grateful now that I own a multimillion-dollar business that I manage easily and effortlessly.

- I'm so happy and grateful now that I am my perfect weight and I live in a healthy, strong body. I have endless energy and feel super proud in my own skin.
- I'm so happy and grateful now that the sky isn't even the limit to what I can do, be or have.
- I'm so happy and grateful now that I now have financial freedom and an ongoing surplus amount of money that keeps increasing month after month after month! This or something better is all I'm willing to accept!

Ella's Story

Ella was extremely frustrated with where she was in her life and business.

She didn't know what to do, and she didn't have a plan.

She had wanted to live the country lifestyle for as long as she could remember. Her love affair with everything country was something she was born with. She grew up on the family property that had belonged to her family for generations.

However, when Ella's father became unwell, the family property was too big to manage and had to be sold. This is when Ella's dreams of taking over the property one day, were destroyed.

Ella knew that her heart belonged in the bush, living, and working the land. She knew that she wanted this lifestyle not only for herself but also for her children and their children.

This was more than just a piece of land to her, this was a way of life, a lifestyle, a deep yearning for her.

Ella decided it was time to turn her childhood dream into reality, but she didn't know where to start. She was currently living over 1000km away from the family block. And was working in an industry so far removed from the lifestyle she knew growing up. Ella was working in coal mining and although it paid the bills, it wasn't what she dreamed of doing or where she dreamed of living.

It felt like this was an impossible dream for her. Ella felt frustrated, and stuck, and had no idea how to turn her dreams into a reality. She was smart, intelligent, and driven, but just didn't know where to start and didn't believe she could get everything she wanted.

After seeing some of my online content, Ella reached out to me and after a conversation, she enrolled in my coaching program. The first thing I did was ask her, 'What do you want?' Ella met this question with a lot of reasons as to why she couldn't have what she wanted.

So, I simply asked her again, 'What do you want?' This time Ella started to open up. She mentioned a few things she wanted, but I knew this was just surface stuff. After asking a third time, it all came out, something she thought she could never have achieved, something she felt would never have come true. Ella said, "I want to own the family farm where I grew up."

And there it was! This was the start of Ella getting what she wanted. At this moment Ella made her first big discovery about goals. She wasn't clear on what she really wanted. Ella mentioned a new car, a nice house a healthy body. But that wasn't what she really wanted. She wanted to own the property that had been in her family for generations. She wanted to live the lifestyle, get her hands dirty and do a hard day's work. She wanted her children to have the same opportunities she had as a kid and have the freedom to explore and experience country living.

After working with Ella for a few months, it became clear to her how she was going to achieve her dream of owning the family farm.

18 months into Ella's coaching journey, I got a phone call from her sharing some exciting news. Her family property had recently come onto the property market, and she had been the successful purchaser! I was so excited for her and knew that this was just the start of how amazing this lady really is.

CHAPTER 4

The Angry Little Rooster

This chapter addresses the key behind why some people succeed and why others fail, plus, why I hate chooks!

I hate chooks! There I've said it, it's out in the open now and it's done! The problem is, I love eating eggs, but chickens are gross and dirty, plus their coop is always smelly and a mess! When you do go to collect the eggs, the chickens will either peck you because they are still sitting on the eggs, or their eggs are covered in poop! It's a gross job and I just don't like chooks.

This love/hate relationship for chooks and their eggs, started when we had a rogue rooster. This rooster thought he was the boss. He would boss the hens around, command respect from the baby chicks and even attack a dog or two if they came anywhere near the chicken coop. He was a vicious little guy, and he knew it. It was so scary going to feed the chooks because you didn't know what mood this rooster was going to be in for that day. Sometimes, he would be all friendly and happy to see you arrive because he knew he was going to get fed. On other days he was an angry little bird and showed you just how angry he could get!

When I was 10 and it was my week of feeding the chooks, I remember walking over there with scrap bucket in hand, nose pinched because of the stench from the scraps and periodically shooing a fly away from my face. I'd made my way over to the chicken coop, which was situated about 100 meters from the house. I walked over the road and onto a little dirt track that led to where the chickens would hang out. The chickens would be out of the coop, happily pecking and scratching at the soil, searching for bugs, grubs, and anything else they found tasty. We were ahead of our time with free-range chickens!

On this particular day as I approached the chicken coop, I looked up to see a very angry, determined little rooster making his way toward me at full speed! I didn't hesitate, I knew he wasn't happy, and I knew he had me in his sights!

Unfortunately, I wasn't quick enough. As he rushed towards me, I dropped the scrap bucket, turned, and started to run as fast as I could. But I was no match for this super-fast, super fierce little rooster who decided he didn't like me on this day! And, before I knew it, he had caught me, and he wasn't going to let me get away. He decided I needed to be taught a lesson. He jumped up and with his spur (the hard, sharp tip at the back of his legs) he dragged it down the back of my leg, scratching me and causing my leg to bleed!

I could feel the sharp pain and quickly glanced down while I continued to run from this beast. I noticed the blood and couldn't hold back the tears and screams. I had just been attacked by a vicious maniac rooster who was after blood! My screaming alerted my mother who thought the worst, that I'd been bitten by a brown snake (another animal to keep an eye out for while walking through long grass, and a lot more dangerous than a rooster). It wasn't until I made it home at record speed that she could see the blood and heard me tell her about the evil rooster through my sobs.

Mum wasn't having it! The good scrap bucket was dumped in the middle of the paddock and that rooster was evil. It was a showdown between my Mum and that wicked rooster! She put on her gumboots and ventured in the direction of the chicken coop. I watched from the front veranda as Mum went confidently towards the chickens who were now pecking at the sprawled-out scraps on the ground.

I was worried for her. I know she had the gumboots on, so that rooster wouldn't be able to scratch her legs. But he was fierce, what if he decided to fly and scratch her face?

Mum got to the bucket and guess what! That rooster was the tamest and quiet I'd ever seen him. He didn't even run at Mum or try any scratching or chasing. He just followed the other chooks as Mum ushered them back into the chicken coop to roost for the night. I couldn't believe how different that rooster was.

What was different between my Mum's approach and mine, you might ask. Mindset. My Mum's mindset was of confidence, determination, and persistence. My mindset was 'A rooster is trying to kill me!' And that rooster could smell it a mile away!

The Key Ingredient

Do you know two people in your life who've had similar upbringings, experiences, and opportunities, but they experience vastly different results in life?

Have you ever noticed that some people appear to have the worst luck while other people will win every meat raffle going? Or when someone is given a cancer diagnosis and decides to give up, while someone else with the same diagnosis, will decides to fight for their life?

If we all start life as a flash of bright light, why do some of us go on to achieve what we want, while others appear to hate every moment of their life?

It comes down to one small difference that has a huge impact! Something you have total control over and no matter what's happened in the past, by understanding this one thing, you can create the future you have always wanted!

So, what is the thing that separates those who thrive in life and those who seem to hit every roadblock along the way? It comes down to this one little but powerful thing once you understand it, you will have the power to create what you want in your own life! What's the difference? What's the magic sauce?

It's your Mindset!

Mindset is the environment you are creating your life from. Mindset is where you plant the seeds of what you want, your dreams, goals, and desires. Mindset is what helps you get emotionally invested in your ideas and then helps you stay persistent in your thoughts and actions to create what you want.

The quality of your mindset will determine the quality of your life.

Have you ever said to yourself:

- I've got to be more positive!
- If only I had more confidence!
- How do I feel more comfortable in my own skin?

If you have ever said any of the above statements, then you know that your mindset needs checking. And just like going to the gym, our mindset is a muscle, and we need to work it regularly. We can't just expect to go to the gym once and walk out like Arnold Schwarzenegger, with huge muscles in ridiculous places. We need to go repetitive times and it may hurt and then we know that the muscle is growing! We don't shower once and think we'll be clean for the rest of our life and so is the same with our mindset. Your mindset is always evolving, and you need to be a guardian, a living example that you can achieve amazing things.

A lot of the time, people think that their mindset is set for the rest of their life. They have tried a few things in the past to change it, but nothing has stuck. They've tried affirmations, they've tried setting a goal, they've tried even changing a habit. And it might work for the short term, but it doesn't seem to work for the long term. It just won't stick. They self-sabotage, procrastinate, talk themselves out of what they want or don't even start, and another week goes by and another and another. It's a repetitive cycle, Groundhog Day, doing the same thing every single day over and over again. You're doing lots of action or lots of 'busy' work, without really completing anything. Just treading water, hoping that something will change, but nothing does. You resign to the belief that the results you're currently getting, are going to be the results you will always get.

However, your mindset isn't fixed. The thoughts you think, and the beliefs you have are not even yours most of the time! That's right. When we are born, we are born a blank slate and we then observe and absorb beliefs, patterns, behaviours, and paradigms from our family, our community, and our culture. We consume messages through TV, books, newspapers, and even the internet. Based on this information, we create our own paradigms or beliefs about ourselves, and this is what forms our mindset. This is the difference between those who have a poverty mindset and those who have a prosperity mindset. The paradigms you choose to believe then become your truth. Our paradigms create the identity of who we believe we are.

So, if you think that you're too old, you're too far gone, there's no hope for you, you've tried and failed so many times in the past...I have GREAT news for you.

It Is NOT too late!

You can re-train, reshape and transform your mindset into anything you want. This might sound too farfetched, but how can anyone in their early 30s to late 70s and beyond, transform their mindset? They've been living that way all their life and they've tried to change in the past, how can they do this in their future? Remember when I said this will sound simple, but it's not always easy? The next activity will highlight this very example. Understanding your mindset and how you can start working in harmony with yourself, instead of against yourself is an integral part of creating the life and business of your dreams! Let's get started!

Action- Affirmations

Affirmations are a powerful strategy that you can use every day to move you closer to achieving your goals, dreams, and desires. To find out more about affirmations go to www.gerryhuston.com.au.

As I said before, it doesn't matter what you've done in the past, or how many times you've failed or given up, this is a fresh start, a line in the sand! And as you're reading this book, I want you to decide that this is you stepping into the version of who you really are. You are learning how to unlock the potential that lies just under the surface within you. And you can do, be and have anything (and I mean ANYTHING), you want.

Bob Proctor would say 'If you can see it in your mind. You will hold it in your hand.'

Meaning, if you have a goal, a desire, or a dream and you infuse emotion into that goal, holding it on the screen of your mind with your will for long enough, then you too will hold that item or achieve that goal in the physical world. You will move it from your conscious mind, from a mere wish or hope to a physical item, attribute, or result.

Everything starts with our thinking. We create from the inside out, and it's so important that you know just how powerful your thoughts are.

I want you to ask yourself a couple of questions to really dig deep and reflect on how you're currently thinking about yourself. Grab a pen and paper and answer the following questions:

- Are your current thoughts positive or negative?
- Do you have empowering thoughts or thoughts that put you down?
- What phrases do you repeat to yourself over and over again?
- How do you feel about yourself?
- What's one thing you wish you would say to yourself, but you're not saying?

I want you to be aware of your internal dialogue because as you'll learn, your thoughts create your results.

Clients have said to me, "Gerry, I've tried affirmations and they just don't work for me." And yes, I've said that in the past too. But every thought you think, every conversation you share, and every phrase you repeat to yourself on more than one occasion is an affirmation. You are affirming what you want (or don't want, but your subconscious mind doesn't know that). Because I'm all about keeping it simple, here is what you need to know to make affirmations work. We have 2 parts to our mind, this isn't the brain, it's the mind that I am talking about here. There is the conscious mind and the subconscious mind. The conscious mind is referred to as our thinking mind and it can accept or reject information. The subconscious mind is our feeling or emotional mind. There is so much reading you can do on these 2 parts of the mind, but I'm going to keep it simple for this explanation. The subconscious mind is the boss, but it can't reject information. So, everything you plant into your subconscious mind MUST be accepted as the truth.

Now, remember I said the thoughts you have, the words you say the phrases you repeat are all affirmations. Even if you say negative words or phrases if you repeat them enough, your subconscious mind will decide that it MUST be the truth of what you want. And because the subconscious mind is a goal-seeking mechanism, it will go about getting you into harmony with thoughts, feelings, and actions toward what you have planted over and over. So, if you're a bully to yourself or have an inner mean girl who always puts you down, guess what's going to happen? Your affirmations are going to be negative, degrading, and derogatory. Go back to the activity where you had to write down what you're currently thinking about yourself. Are you a bully or a friend to you?

Here are some powerful Affirmations you can write and repeat daily:

- I love and respect myself
- Everything is working out for me
- I am so organised

- I am a Powerful being
- I easily achieve my goals
- I am an energetic match for miracles
- I am surrounded by love
- I have deep loving relationships
- Being disciplined is so easy
- I am so grateful for my life
- It's so easy to make money
- I make money while I sleep
- I am a money magnet
- I love my life

Once you've chosen two or three powerful affirmations, you will need to plant the seed of what you want. Remember from Chapter 1 when I talked about what seeds you are planting in the soil of your mindset? Goals and Affirmations are the seeds of what you want. It's impossible to think of two opposing thoughts at the exact same time. You might jump between a negative and positive thought quickly, but you can't hold a negative thought and a positive thought simultaneously. Therefore, you can focus on your affirmations knowing that the opposite of what it is you want, won't pop up during this time.

Autosuggestion is the best way to water your affirmations and make sure they grow in the subconscious mind. Here are a few examples of how to autosuggest:

- Writing your affirmations daily
- Saying your affirmations in the mirror morning and night
- Listening to your affirmations on repeat throughout your day

However, the best way to plant those affirmations is to become emotionally connected to them. So, when you've chosen an affirmation, imagine you're already in possession of what it represents to you. How does that feel? Exciting, happy, joyful, proud, fun, prosperous, abundant, or peaceful. Stay connected to that feeling as long as possible throughout your day, and magic will happen!

Tania's Story

When I first started working with Tania, she said something that really stuck with me.

During Tania's Orientation session, we were going through the Life Audit questions and really getting a gauge for where she was in her life at that stage. We discussed what was working, what wasn't working, and what she wanted to achieve in her life and business.

Tania was a widow who was running a rural family business with her adult son. Tania was navigating this new role and shift in power, going from discussing everything with her husband, to ultimately being the key stakeholder who has the final say. The buck stopped with her!

Tania said to me on that day, "I want to be the captain of my own ship." For far too long, the needs of the business, extended family members, and everything else had gone before her own interests, dreams, and goals. And the stress of this had taken its toll. Tania is one of the kindest and most caring people you'll meet, she is beautiful inside and out. So, this shift in circumstance was an unexpected curve ball that life had thrown at her.

That's when we started focusing on what Tania wanted. Not what she thought she should do now, but what she actually wanted for herself. That's when Tania lit up and shared that she'd always wanted to be a helicopter pilot but thought she wouldn't have the fortitude or confidence to fly. This is where I shared with her the importance of mindset and creating a mindset that supports your goals, not one that works against you. So, from now on, Tania was going to become her biggest cheerleader, her own raving fan. She was going to only focus on what she wanted and see herself achieving it all.

Tania began by choosing a few key affirmations that supported her in her goals and allowed her to stretch beyond what she felt was possible. I encouraged Tania to have her affirmations displayed around her house and workspace, so she would see them regularly. Tania also had her affirmations on voice loop on her phone and would listen to them in the background when working. All of these little steps allowed her to positively autosuggest her goal and rewire her mindset.

I witnessed Tania blossom as her passion to become a pilot grew. Tania was more than capable of achieving anything she put her mind to, she just needed the help and guidance to get started and a roadmap to help set her mindset up in a positive way.

I'm proud to say, that it's now two years later and Tania has completed her study and is flying high. Tania went from wanting to be the captain of her own ship, to the pilot of her life!

CHAPTER 5

Why Shetland Ponies are the Psychopaths of the Horse World and What That Means for You!

If nothing changes on the inside, you won't have a long-term positive change on the outside. This chapter will highlight the important strategy that I witnessed from every Shetland Pony I've ever met, to help make internal positive change on a deep level!

I have never met a Shetland Pony I liked! I've grown up riding lots of different ponies and horses throughout my life. Here's my list of a few of them:- Jay, who was a tall bay beautiful mare. Midnight, whose coat was nearly white, but a very long time before he was my horse, was jet black in colour. Windfield, (yes named after the cigarette company, not very politically correct in the '80s) was a beautiful stock horse and then my favourite pony named Dolly who was all belly and a fabulous kids pony because of her kind nature.

As kids, we also had a variety of Shetland Ponies and none of them were very nice at all. I like to refer to Shetland Ponies as the psychopaths of the horse world! They trick you into thinking they are kind because they look so darn cute. Their cute little stocky round bellies, lovely fluffy coats, oversized heads with those big, beautiful eyes, that make you melt whenever you look in their direction. But don't be fooled. I have one very clear memory of my older sister Gaye, being placed on one of these devils in disguise when she was twelve. Once she had climbed onto this miniature master mind's back, that Shetland took off like a rocket across the paddock with my sister holding on for dear life! To Gaye's credit, she rode that little Shetland well. I'm not sure who was more determined that day.

As soon as you go to catch one of these little Shetlands, they turn evil! They dodge, dart away and have the manoeuvres of an elite football player! Some would say that the Shetland Pony has moves like Muhammad Ali's "Float like a butterfly, sting like a bee." Once you do finally corner them and they realise they have no place to go, they reluctantly allow you to approach them, but not without one final attempt to get past! You know this is a bluff, so you hold your ground, and they finally give in to being caught. You lovingly brush their whole body, but instead of being grateful, they try stepping on your toes or pushing you away by leaning on you, knocking you off balance. Even if you did remove that burr that's been stuck in their fluffy hair and probably annoying them for weeks, they really don't care or show any gratitude.

Once the saddle goes on, they blow their stomach out so much, that the girth that holds the saddle on the horse, only just fits. You scratch your head, wondering how this little pony has put on so much weight since the last ride! Once you've squeezed the girth clasp closed, you walk the little guy around to make sure the saddle is fit properly. Because horses can't hold their breath for that long, once the walk is completed, you successfully tighten the girth up, noticing their tummy has reduced significantly.

Everyone's got their horses ready and waiting for you, so you hop on to your little Shetland Pony and think it's going to be a great ride. However, that little sweet horse has a psychopathic mind! Its only aim for this ride is to get rid of YOU. Every low-hanging tree that the pony sees, guess what, it drags you under! Having to lean all the way back lying down flat on the back of the horse as the branches scratch your face. Every gate you go through, deliberately walks close to the post, rubbing your leg raw on the fence. Every puddle or waterhole, your shetland thinks it's a submarine and starts submerging itself into the body of water, trying to shake you off in the process. You cling on for dear life, just hoping you don't get too wet, or your Shetland decides that this is the perfect time for a roll in the mud! Yep, Shetland Ponies are the psychopaths of the horse world. Give me a Clydesdale any day!

But we can all learn a thing or two from our little Shetland Pony frenemies! These little ponies see themselves as the most important thing in the paddock, actually the most important thing on the whole property, including more important than you!

- They will happily challenge any other horse for the boss role, even though the other horses are three times their size! If they're not the boss, they soon will be!
- Fences are just a suggestion to the Shetland Pony. They use it as a guide but not as enforcement. If there's something they want in the next paddock next door, there is no wire too low for them to Houdini their way past, through, or over.
- And the way they carry themselves. They have little horse syndrome! Only stand at about one meter in height, but still, see themselves as six-foot tall and dingo-proof!

Wouldn't we all benefit from a little bit of Shetland Pony's self-confidence? Wouldn't we all benefit from seeing ourselves just like those stubborn little Shetland Ponies see themselves? They see themselves as the boss of all, the one in charge, as the King of their (and everyone else's) lives!

I'll Be Happy When…

Have you ever had a time in your life when you felt less than perfect? And if you're human, you would have answered a big fat 'YES' to that question. It's really normal to not be our biggest fans every minute of the day. However, if you're wanting to change your life for the better, achieve a BIG goal (or really any goal), transform your business, or improve your life, then you've got to start on the inside first. You've got to be a bit more like the Shetland Pony, seeing yourself as worthy, amazing, and extremely important!

I used to hate mirrors! I would always avoid looking at myself in the mirror and hated gyms that had full lengths mirrors or hairdressers where you're sat staring straight at your own reflection staring back at you. On a very odd occasion or as I rushed to put my makeup on in the morning, I'd look in the mirror, but my eyes were always drawn to the perceived flaws I saw in my appearance. My belly was too jiggly and wobbly, my double chins were noticeable, that blotchy red skin on my cheeks was really showing and the list went on and on and on! Whenever I caught my reflection, I'd pick at my flaws, put myself down, and consequently feel terrible about myself for the rest of the day. I didn't want to go outside. I didn't want to socialise. I felt so uncomfortable in my own skin, I didn't even want people to look at me!

This shouldn't be happening to me! I'd done so much personal development on myself. I shouldn't be STILL hitting up against these negative feelings. After all, I'm a strong, independent woman, I don't need validation from anyone to feel good about myself. The real issue was, I was my own worst enemy. It wasn't even a frenemy situation. I hated myself.

I hated the way I looked, the way I appeared to others, and certain parts of my body and because of that, I found it so difficult to unconditionally love the person within. And it didn't only affect my appearance, I started putting my own achievements down, I started focusing on my weaknesses and my failures. I would look at my business and beat myself up for not being better, doing better, making more money, having more clients, and having more of a social media following. Then it started to ripple into every other aspect of my life; my friendships, my relationship with my husband, my parenting style, and worst of all, how I would think, feel, and talk about myself. The things I would say to myself, I would NEVER say that to my worst enemy. I had an inner mean girl that was an absolute b*tch! And what I used to do, was justify that once I had achieved something, then I would be happy.

I used to say to myself:

- When I lose weight, then I'll be happy.
- When I get into a size 12 pair of jeans, then I'll love myself.
- When I'm making big money in my business, then I'll feel successful.
- I'll be happy when…..

In the past, I'd done so much with my mindset, learning about paradigms, positive thinking, breaking the cycle, inner child work, energy healing, and affirmations, but it felt like I was taking two steps forward and three steps back! As important as all of that is, there was still a piece missing and I couldn't put my finger on what it was!

No matter how hard I tried, I was always hitting up the same old roadblocks. I just felt like I was coasting through life and no matter what I did, nothing seemed to improve, or it improved for a short time, then I'd go right back to get the same results as before!

Let me give you an example. Each month I'd make roughly the same amount of money in my business. And then one month I'd make significantly more money than I had the previous months, I was ecstatic. But it was short-lived. Because come the following month, I'd be back to the same amount or less than before. This is what I call my money set point. We all have set points for different areas of our lives.

We have set points for:

- The money we make
- The love we receive
- Our level of health
- Our weight
- How successful we are in our business
- And many other areas

I also noticed this with my husband. The conversations would be either about money and how we were spending it, or who cleaned the house last and how unfair that was! We would fight about the same things over and over again. I just felt like I was blocked and stuck.

Our set point is a belief in the level of success we think we deserve, and this is usually an unconscious thing to us. Say, for example, if we have continually made $5000 income per month for a long period of time, you can extrapolate, that $5000 is the set point. However, if in one particular month the income goes up to $7000, in the following months, the income will most likely go back to the set point of $5000, because the inside work hasn't been done to create long-term positive change. The set point is like an autopilot, helping you stay on course and in harmony with the beliefs you have about the success you feel you deserve.

Once I noticed my set points, I was furious! I could see the patterns I had repeated in my life over and over again. I'd lose the weight and then I'd put it all back on and MORE! I'd make the money for a short term but would be back at my set point income quicker than I'd like to admit. I could never break past my self-imposed set points and have the abundant business, the sexy body, and the happy relationships I wanted. I was stuck, miserable, and confused as to why I wasn't progressing.

Activity: Self-Image Is The Answer

It was like a lightbulb went off inside of me when I heard about a term called self-image. I didn't really give it much thought before because self-image sounded like it involved mirrors, and you know how much I hated mirrors!

However, self-image was a term Maxwell Maltz, a plastic surgeon, coined in the 1960s. He would notice after doing cosmetic surgery on people, to help with their disfigurements, that some people would be more confident, more successful, and live happier lives. While others, even though their physical appearance had changed, they still felt like they carried the disfigurements from their past. He observed that there are two images that we hold of ourselves. The first image is the image we project to the outside world, how we want people to see us. That involves the clothes we wear, how we talk, how we walk, how we hold ourselves, the makeup we use, the way we style our hair even our mannerisms. The other image is our inner self-image, how we think, feel, and what we believe about ourselves.

Self-image determines those feelings we feel about ourselves, the words we say, that inner voice, the way we treat ourselves, and the beliefs that we have about who we believe we are. Self-image is the picture we hold on the inside. When we examine our results, we can determine how successful we will be in all areas of our life, based on our self-image. So, changing the results you get on the outside, is an inside job. You must change the image, feelings, beliefs, and paradigms you have of yourself, before anything on the outside will change. As Sandy Gallagher says, 'You can't outperform a poor self-image.' Once you've got your self-image on track, you've got your life on track.

Self-image is a very powerful tool for determining our future results. Why is this so, you may ask? It's because whatever we have planted in our subconscious mind, must come to fruition.

I love Bob Proctor's quote 'If you can see it in your mind. You will hold it in your hand.'

So, if you have an image of yourself where you are lacking in confidence, feel limited by what you think you can achieve, are negative about most things, or have a poverty mentality, then, your subconscious mind will actively seek that out. Because your subconscious mind is in alignment with the self-image you have, (even if it's not what you want) your subconscious is so powerful and will draw that into your physical world as a result. Until you closely examine your self-image, you probably don't know what your self-image holds. Your self-image is heavily influenced by the thoughts you have, the feelings you get into harmony with, and the actions you take.

Let's dig a bit deeper here and really nut out how this relates to the Shetland Ponies that I grew up with as a kid. Shetland Ponies see themselves as the biggest horse in the paddock, the boss of the mob, six foot tall, and bulletproof. If they hit up against an obstacle, they just find a way around it, or in the case of a fence, they find their way under it! There is no rider who gets the better of them. They have an arsenal of tricks in their back pocket to rid any rider who dares to stay on longer than welcome. Pig rooting, kicking out, rolling, scraping under trees, walking where they shouldn't be, or even resorting to shaking their rider off! We could take a tip or two from the psychopaths of the horse world, the Shetland Ponies.

Now, let's create a successful self-image of your very own. Firstly, you've got to get clear on what it is you really want. If you don't know what you want, it's like getting in your car and deciding you want to go for a drive, but you don't even know where you want to drive. So, you reverse out of the garage and onto the street. Then, you drive back into the garage. Then, you reverse back out onto the street and then drive back into the garage. You're doing a lot of action but getting no real result. The key is to get really clear on what it is you want. What is your dream, your goal right now? If you could do, be or have anything, what would it be?

I get my clients to let their imaginations run wild with this one! It's time to have fun, to connect back with your childhood dreams and your desires. If you're having trouble breaking through the 'reality bubble' you've placed on yourself or talking yourself out of your goals, even before you've written them down. Ask yourself this question and write down what flows;

> 'When everything is possible, what would I love?'

Also, refer to the previous chapter for help with identifying and writing your goal. Or find more Self-Image resources at www.gerryhuston.com.au

Secondly, once you've identified what it is you want, I want you to create a list of characteristics and attributes of the person who's already achieved that goal. Much like the self-image of a confident, headstrong Shetland Pony, you'll create your list of what you want. Ask yourself:

'Who do I need to become to achieve this?'

What would the thoughts of the person who's already achieved these goals be? She/he isn't putting themselves down, they're not moping about feeling sorry for themselves or thinking negative and limiting thoughts. This person is thinking empowering, motivational, and positive thoughts. This person is your biggest cheerleader and is cheering you on through everything!

How would you be feeling as this person, who has achieved everything they want? Would you be happy, calm, satisfied, excited, peaceful, easy-going, fun, relaxed, intentional, focused, or loving?

Write down a couple of feelings that really stood out to you. And you can create *I am* statements with these feeling words.

For example:

- I am happy
- I am confident and calm
- I am peaceful
- I am a go-getter

- I am relaxed and in flow
- am love

Finally, the last step towards creating a Shetland Pony self-image is to apply action. If you're not putting action behind this, then nothing will change in the long term.

From here, what actions does this confidence, go-getter, powerful person take? Do they take actions that move them closer to achieving their goals, and if so, what are those actions? Does this person work smarter not harder? Is this person productive and persistent? Really have fun with this one and draw out all the actions you would take as this person. Remembering, that you have the thoughts and feelings that support this new self-image. So, get a bit creative with your actions. If you're needing help with this step, just look at the great leaders, entrepreneurs, minds, and influences of today. Do you think Elon Musk would action his ideas or procrastinate? Really check in and see what or who else inspires you and draw on their experiences.

Examples of Actions:

- Schedule or time block your day
- Follow up on leads
- Make those important calls
- Write down 3 to 6 Goal Achieving Actions daily and complete them
- Reward yourself for actions you have taken
- Follow your intuitive guidance

Bree's Story

When I first met Bree, she struck me as being one of the most beautiful people I've met, both on the outside, and more importantly, such a beautiful person on the inside! Bree would do anything for a friend, was kind and thoughtful, but always put herself last. She had no idea of just how awesome a person she was!

I hazard a guess that, if you're reading this book, you're probably a little bit like my client Bree too. Never giving yourself credit for just how amazing you really are.

People who were in Bree's life would compliment her regularly on how much of a great friend and how awesome she was. However, Bree never acknowledged these compliments and always thought the worst of herself. She didn't see herself as an amazing, talented, or even valuable person. She held a self-image of being broken, and life (as it does) gave her evidence as to why this was the case. She was unhappy in her job and felt underappreciated and undervalued. Bree had given so much to everyone else, however, forgot about herself and her needs along the way.

After Bree saw me speak, she approached me to see if coaching would be a fit for her. We had a conversation and she enrolled in my coaching program; for Bree, the breakthroughs started to happen quickly.

We worked on Bree's self-image eliminating how she currently saw herself and creating a new abundant and successful self-image. Bree started to realise her worth and instead of seeing herself as broken, she started to appreciate the little things and have gratitude for herself. Bree realised her boundaries were being pushed in her job and she was underappreciated. So, she applied for another job and got it. Plus, this job was four times what she was getting paid in her previous position. Bree started doing little things for herself. She started wearing lipstick, doing meditation, and even going on retreats for herself.

It's been such a gift to see Bree flourish and blossom! Bree is a reminder to us all; If nothing changes on the inside, nothing changes on the outside!

CHAPTER 6

Your Attitude Determines Your Altitude

This is one of the best-kept secrets of how to overcome a negative or limiting mindset every single time! It's also a very simple activity that will have you transforming your results quickly.

You can tell pretty quickly who's going to make it living in the bush and who's not cut out for the long days of isolation, hard work, and mental strength it takes to overcome the hardships experienced on a regular basis. A lot of people think living on the land is glamorous and idealistic. Don't get me wrong, I loved my childhood and being able to have the freedom of growing up in the middle of nowhere, able to ride, explore and grow. However, it wasn't always the ideal scene it's portrayed in some movies or on people's Instagram feeds.

A lot of the time while I was growing up, we were a plaything to the weather conditions. Our feelings were dictated by the season we were having. Let me explain.

When we had a good season, it meant the rain was plentiful, the grass was green, the dams were full of water and the cattle were fat and happy. When it was a good season, everyone was happy. Not just my family, but most of the people in our community were also happy. You'd go to tennis days or BBQs at the neighbours and the mood was happy, light, laughter, and cheers. Everything just felt alive and abundant. Water and grass were plentiful, and the feeling of gratitude was contagious!

However, there were other times, when we wouldn't have rain or much rain for years. This is when the grass started to go brown and die until you started having more patches of dirt than grass in the paddocks. The cattle started to get poorly, and you could see their hip bones protruding more and more each day. Water became a precious commodity, and any evidence of wastage (a longer shower than a couple of minutes, leaving the tap running while brushing our teeth, or unnecessary watering of the garden), would create an outburst from a parent telling you to not waste water! This is also when the community felt tired and sad, and the stench of worry would penetrate every social occasion. There was a worry about how to pay loans, how to pay for feed to keep animals alive, and how to provide for your family. And because we lived where we worked, we were surrounded by it day after day.

Every drop of rain, no matter how small, was measured and mulled over. The amount was shared with neighbours and family members and we either celebrated because we had the most or berated because there wasn't enough. An overcast day bought excitement and anticipation that today was going to be the day that the sky would open and down would come that precious wet gold to soak the earth and the grass would grow!

It was amazing how much of our life was consumed and dictated by either a good or a bad season. We knew when it was ok to jump on the trampoline with the hose and water splashing everywhere, or when this behaviour would definitely result in getting a smack!

My parents have always been on the land. They both grew up on properties and have been living in the bush ever since. It was one particularly harsh drought, only about 5 years ago, when the rain just didn't seem like it was coming, and the dams were getting dry. The Summer rains that usually broke the drought just weren't around and the endless blue skies reiterated how relentless things had become. I reluctantly asked my parents how they were feeling about the drought and the continuous evaporation of water every day. What surprised me was my Mum's response, saying, 'It'll rain one day!'

There was no negativity, no worry, or fear. I asked her to repeat herself because I thought I'd miss heard. As a kid, the lack of rain was a major stressor for my parents. However, to hear my mum reply like this, I had to know more. Mum repeated herself and told me it's all about your attitude. If you don't have the right attitude, you'll be focusing on what you don't want, instead of on what you do want. So, every day, was a day closer to rain.

When the Birds and Bees are Challenging

Growing up on a property, you get to know how animals make more animals pretty quickly. The birds and bees talk really doesn't have to happen, or it happens very young. You witness it happening in your own real-life classroom just by being surrounded by all those animals. Much like death is something that country kids are exposed to at a very young age. So, when it came to starting our own family, I thought it was going to happen SO quickly and easily. Boy was I wrong!

My husband and I struggled for years with infertility issues. We had tried the herbs, the spices, the exploratory operations, making love on certain days, the moon cycle, buying a white couch, going on a holiday, losing weight, putting on muscle, both distracting and focusing on ourselves, attending courses, reading books, watching documentaries, taking medications, seeing Doctors, Acupuncturists, Masseuse, Herbalists, Kinesiologists, Reiki Masters, Naturopaths, talking with friends, listening to family members and hearing from everyone what they think we need to do to fall pregnant.....we tried EVERYTHING!

We did it all, heard it all, and tried it all! Been there, done that, and got the t-shirt to prove it! I was a farm kid, so having children was just a rite of passage and should've been EASY! I'd witness how effortless it was for the farm animals, for our family members, and for my friends to fall pregnant and fulfill their dreams of being parents.

Being on the infertility journey for five years really took its toll. I had gone from a bubbly, outgoing, and positive person to becoming withdrawn, bitter, and resentful, feeling like a failure. I felt like my body was broken! I couldn't get pregnant and worst of all, we were categorised as having *Unexplained Infertility*! I was constantly reminded of what a failure I felt like, every time I walked into my classroom of students and saw children, the thing I was so desperate to have in my own life.

Tim, my husband was a beacon of light throughout this entire experience. Although it was tough on him too, he always looked for the positive. After five years of 'trying' to fall pregnant, we were told our only option was IVF. IVF wasn't what we wanted to do; I don't think many people want to do IVF. Tim suggested we start thinking about this in a totally different way. He recommended we change our attitude. I took his lead, and we both decided to metaphorically draw a line in the sand. Whatever had happened in the past, was not going to be dragged into our future.

The attitude we decided to have when we started our IVF journey was *'Whatever will be. Will be.'* Throughout this whole ordeal and as tough as it was, Tim and I became closer, more connected, and a strong united team.

This won't surprise anybody, but IVF was not fun! I had daily injections, mood swings, bloating, and times when I felt like I was hit by a bus. However, we considered ourselves the lucky ones. Because after a fresh transfer of a precious little embryo, our eight-week scan showed a strong heartbeat! It felt like we had been holding our breaths for eight weeks while waiting to see if our embryo had or hadn't made it! Nine months later, we were overjoyed with the safe arrival of a nine-pound healthy and noisy baby boy! He had jet black hair, cute chubby cheeks, and was extremely vocal, letting the whole world know he was here. I fell in love instantly and knew from there that this was one of my proudest moments, being his mum.

Activity: Attitude Template

Access your Attitude Template at www.gerryhuston.com.au

You might have noticed that this chapter is full of the secret sauce to change your mindset. Yes, you guessed it, Attitude!

Attitude is more than if you've just got a good or bad attitude. Attitude is the whole person. And once you understand the attitude, you will see a huge difference in your experiences, results, and whole life.

Growing up, we were always told to have a good, positive attitude and that was how we'd get ahead in life. But, as a kid, I had no idea what this meant! Even as an adult, I had a rudimentary understanding of what attitude was, but I still had no idea how to create a super kick-arse winning attitude or even how to create success.

I thought that having a positive attitude meant that you said positive things or did positive actions. You smiled at strangers, you gave compliments to your friends and work colleagues, or you were polite.

Attitude is deeper, it's more of a holistic approach. And once you understand your attitude, you will have a tool that will help you in every area of your life. Access your Attitude Template at www.gerryhuston.com.au

You can create attitudes for so many different parts of your life:

- Confidence
- Parenting
- Business
- Negotiations
- Sales

- Relationship
- Friendship
- Success
- Money

Attitude is more than just surface level; it goes beyond what you simply think or feel or do. It's the combination of these 3 areas:

1. Your thoughts
2. Your feelings
3. Your actions

It's the combination of these three areas that make long-lasting positive change. Here's how it works.

Thoughts:

Your thoughts are the starting place for your attitude. If you think negative, lacking, unhappy thoughts, you're going to create a negative, unhappy, and ungrateful attitude.

Feelings:

Feelings are an important part of attitude. You can be demonstrating on the outside the actions of a positive person. But, unless you're feeling positive, you won't be fooling anyone. You must FEEL it before you BE it! The feeling is the key.

Actions:

What actions are you demonstrating to the world, from your current attitude? The thoughts you think, create pictures in your mind. You become emotionally connected to those pictures with feeling. These feelings inspire you to act, further demonstrating to the outside world your attitude.

The first thing you need to do, to create the attitude you want, is to be super honest with yourself and where you are right now!

Decide which area of your life you're going to focus on first. It might be parenting, confidence, relationships, work, or anything that's currently not going the way you want it to be.

Once you've chosen the area, you're going to create a new attitude around it, you then need to write three headings: - Thoughts, Feelings, and Actions. Beside each heading give yourself a score between 1 and 10 reflecting your current attitude. 1 meaning you have a terrible, negative horrible attitude for this area of your life. 10 meaning you have a rockstar, positive, outstandingly awesome attitude.

For Example:

Current Confidence Attitude

Thoughts- 4/10

Feelings- 3/10

Actions- 3/10

Be honest…is it a 5/10 because you're sometimes positive, and sometimes negative in your thinking. Or is it more like a 2/10 because you know you've been your own worst bully and erode your confidence on a continual basis? This is not an opportunity to judge yourself, put yourself down, or beat yourself up. I want you to be impartial when you are completing this first part! I want you to notice it but know that this isn't who you truly are. You wouldn't be reading this book if you didn't believe, (even deep down) that you were meant for more! More greatness, more love, more money, etc.

The next step is to write down your current thoughts, the things you continually say or think to yourself. Followed by your current feelings and current actions.

For example:

Current Confidence Attitude

Thoughts- 4/10

- I'm not good enough
- I'll never be as confident as I want
- What do I know

Feelings- 3/10

- Worry
- Stress
- Frustrated

Actions- 3/10

- Never contribute to conversations, I'll always listen.
- Worry about what other people think, so I don't go out as much as I'd like.
- Self-sabotage my dreams and goals.

Look at your answers, remember not to judge, just be the observer. This is your starting point. This is your line in the sand moment! You are changing your attitude from where you are now, to what you want it to be!

NOW, let's shake that old attitude out of the way. As Taylor Swift likes to sing, 'Shake It Off!' Put this book down now and shake it off! Go on, do it!

You're all shaken off! Brilliant, now let's create a 10/10 Attitude! Grab yourself another piece of paper and start with the heading- My New Confidence Attitude (or whatever area you were working on previously). Then go through the same activity, but instead of where you currently are, what would your new attitude look like if it was a 10/10 attitude?

My New Confidence Attitude

Thoughts- I want you to think about what thoughts this 10/10 attitude person would have.

- I can and I am
- I am strong

- I am confident
- I can achieve anything I put my mind to

Feelings- what feelings would your 10/10 Attitude have?

- Happy
- Confident
- Outgoing
- Strong

Actions- What actions would move you forward, and keep you in this rockstar 10/10 attitude?

- Contributing to conversations
- Reminding myself that: - what other people think of me is none of my business.
- Doing one small thing every week that puts me out of my comfort zone.
- Visualising myself as a confident person

Now, what I want you to do, is put that worksheet on your wall or somewhere, where you'll see it regularly. I want you to immerse yourself into this attitude by actioning the steps you've written down one at a time (you might choose to do one of the actions weekly until you feel it starting to be your new normal). Remember now you have the thoughts, feelings, and actions of your ideal 10/10 attitude right there in front of you.

Jacko's Story

My Dad, Jacko has the best attitude of anyone I know. And it's not because life has been easy for him, or everything has worked out perfectly and he's had no speedbumps along the way. It's because he works on his attitude every day of his life.

Jacko suffered great loss and grief in his early 20s, and most people who'd experienced what he went through, would have been crippled, eternally devastated, or unable to go on. However, not Jacko. Don't get me wrong, he grieved and mourned the loss, but he never let it define the rest of his life.

Growing up, Jacko talked about what had happened to him in his early life and how he addressed it. To begin with, he admitted it did involve a lot of drinking to numb his pain and sorrow. Then, there came a time when he knew something needed to change. And that's when he made a choice. He made a choice to look forward. He had a young daughter who was relying on him, a family business to keep running, and cattle in the paddocks. He was also a young man, who had the rest of his life ahead of him and he could choose to stay stuck in the grief and sorrow or choose to take one small step.

Jacko decided to take one small step each day, looking for something small that was good, working on his attitude, and showing up each day. He chose positivity, faith, and gratitude as his new attitude. Looking for the positive in every situation. Having faith that his life would get better. And grateful for his family and friends who supported him throughout the toughest days of his life.

If you're ever lucky enough to meet Jacko, you'll be meeting a man with the biggest heart of anybody I know, the best and brightest smile, and a good yarn to go with it! He has a hunger for life and loves meeting new people. There is never a place he goes where he doesn't know someone or makes a connection and a lifelong friend.

His amazing attitude has rubbed off on me also. I remember my father saying to me, 'You've got to have a great attitude in life."

So, I took his advice and applied it to all areas of my own life, my career, relationships, friendships, business, and even parenting. This has opened so many doors for me because when you have a positive attitude, it's contagious. Even when I've hit up against adversities, tough times, and road bumps, I've always remembered Dad's advice to look for the good stuff, look for the growth and always check in with your attitude.

I am eternally grateful to Jacko for teaching me how important attitude is. Love you Dad xo

CHAPTER 7

Tame the Wild Beast

What I learned from stretching
outside of my comfort zone during
one school holiday on the farm.

When I was sixteen, I was given the fun holiday activity of breaking in my first horse! Breaking in a horse is where you take a young horse that's never been handled by humans or ridden before and gain its trust, teaching it new skills until you can eventually catch it, saddle it, and ride it.

My horse was a chestnut gelding that was just four years old and was called Ginger. He wasn't fully grown, but in saying that, he was still twelve hands high (I don't know why they measure horses in hands still to this day, but if you imagine an average-sized horse, you'll have an accurate picture of how tall Ginger was). Imagine an untamed 500kg chestnut male horse that's never been around humans before!

So, each day of the school holidays, I'd head down to the yards and teach Ginger a new skill. We would build trust, and I'd get him used to being around humans and growing a connection with each other. I was sh*t scared of this giant horse! I wasn't a very confident rider, especially if they were fast! I hated show rides, rollercoasters, or heights, and once was restricted from going on a show ride because I was too tall for this baby merry-go-round! It was mortifying! Anyway, you get the picture of me not being an adrenaline junkie! I loved the opposite, a calm, peaceful horse ride with very reliable, slightly older horses.

As each day of the breaking-in goes on, you get closer and closer to being able to ride your horse. Starting with being able to catch your horse, putting a halter on them, then a saddle blanket, followed by a saddle (but not done up yet). Then progress to a girth done up. After the horse feels comfortable, you'll just put your weight in the stirrups and start pulling yourself up, but not completely get on the horse. You keep going through this gradual process over about three to four weeks until you can confidently climb onto the horse and ride it firstly in a yard and then in an open paddock.

I was petrified and scared to have my first ride! I'd grown up around horses all my life, and I'd seen what horses could do!

They could:

- Buck you off
- Pig root
- Roll with you on their back
- Kickout
- Buck, pig root, kick out, and roll all together!

I was so scared. I kept asking my dad if he'd like the honour of the first ride (I was thoughtful like that)! He wasn't falling for my tricks and saw straight through my nerves and fear. He also knew I was capable of doing this; all I had to do was just stretch outside my comfort zone.

Needless to say, I wasn't pleased with this experience. I wanted to do what other kids did on their holidays, hang out with friends, go to the movies, and go swimming. But, no, I grew up on a farm, and my holiday fun activity was breaking in a 500kg wild beast!

I stepped through each of the stages with my horse, and as

the days were growing, so was my confidence in myself and my abilities. Ginger was becoming more trusting of me, and I was becoming more trusting of him. We finally got to the day when Dad felt I would be able to mount my newly broken-in horse. I was SH*TTING myself (not literally, but close). I was fine doing all the groundwork, but once I was up in that saddle, the ground looked a LONG way away. As it was, the first time I got on Ginger, Dad was on a very calm and quiet horse, also in the pen with me. This comforted me, but I was still afraid of falling off and hurting myself.

I took a deep breath as I held the reins in one hand and put my foot in the stirrup while using my other hand to help pull me up into the saddle. Even at this stage, it still wasn't too late for me to back out, I wasn't entirely up on Ginger's back, and I could decide that this was a training exercise and I wasn't going to jump on him.

However, I could feel Dad's horse holding close to me, only giving me enough room to slide up between his horse and mine. He was in preparation, holding onto my horse's reins, too, just in case Ginger decided to take off. This was SO difficult, that couple of seconds between not wanting to do it, but my body getting into motion and following through with the action anyway and climbing into the saddle for the first time! This was fu*king scary.

I was up there. I was still scared but optimistic and felt accomplished. Ginger wasn't sure what was happening now, but he wasn't doing a combination of bucking, pig-rooting, rolling, or back kicks. This felt like a win! Until Ginger took fright (got scared) and realised I was actually staying on his back, not hopping down like the other times, he started moving around quickly. Luckily with my Dad's help and the groundwork I put in previously, this subsided quickly, and Ginger soon relaxed into having me stay on his back.

Now, don't get me wrong, it's not like he was perfect for every other ride after that one time! No way! He was flighty the next couple of times. He even needed a lot of leading around the yard to calm down. And yes, he did pig root and kicked out, but he never bucked me off!

So, what did breaking in Ginger teach me? That whole experience taught me that your comfort zone is the only thing keeping you blocked, small and stuck. If I didn't push through my comfort zone and break through the fear and terror I was feeling; I would never have had a beautiful horse to ride, and I would have always been at that same level, never progressing. We think our comfort zone is keeping us safe, secure, and avoiding risks! But what it's doing is allowing our wild beast to get away with whatever it wants to get away with. When we jump on that wild beast, break out of our comfort zone, and do the things that make us scared, (face the fear), that's when real living, and really understanding ourselves comes to life!

Why We Always Give In To Our Excuses

You've let yourself dream a little bit. You've identified your goal, the thing that lights you up. You've then stretched that gaol, so it's bigger, juicier, and more exciting. You light up thinking about it. It sends a tingle of excitement throughout your entire body! You can see what you want; it's glorious, it's magnificent, it's everything you've ever wanted. You know that when you achieve this dream, goal, or desire, your life will be glorious, wonderful, unique, and exciting. You will feel happy, joyful, peaceful, prosperous, but most importantly, proud of yourself. Proud knowing that you created this, worked for it, and attracted this magnificent thing into your life that once felt impossible, felt like it would always stay as a dream, nothing tangible, nothing real. Then reality hits you!

- I can't do that
- I'll never succeed
- Who am I to think I can do, be or have that
- I'm so selfish, wanting that
- It's too much; what will people think
- What will people say when I fail
- I don't have the time
- I don't have the skills
- I'm too old, fat, young, thin, dumb, uneducated (insert any insult here)
- This can't happen to me
- I'm too busy now
- It's too hard to get what I want
- I've never done this before, so I won't be able to do this in the future
- Life is too hard

- Life is meant to be difficult
- I will never get what I want

We end up giving in to our excuses and providing oxygen to why we can't do something. Here, let's test this out. If I asked you, 'Do you think you can make a million dollars today?'

What's the first thing you say to yourself?

- Fu*k off
- I'd love to, but I can't.
- As if! That's ridiculous!
- I've never done that, and I never will!
- No, I can't, it's impossible!
- Tell her she's dreaming (that's a Castle reference for all my Aussies aged over 30)

Usually, it's about the first or second thing people tend to think about when it comes to a goal: how they CAN'T do it! How impossible it is, or how ridiculous they were for even thinking they could do it in the first place! I've found myself doing this when I'm about to embark on a big, hairy, scary, exciting goal. Most people talk themselves out of their plan, even before they begin. They give oxygen to their excuses and reasons why they can't do, be or have what they want!

Think back throughout your life when you had a goal, dream, or desire, and you talked yourself out of it! You might have:

- Stopped yourself from traveling overseas and working because you feared the unknown.
- You stayed in a job, or a relationship WAY longer than you should have!
- Didn't start your business, even though you knew you wanted to and knew you'd be amazing at it!
- You didn't take that leap of faith because you were worried about what people would think.
- You pulled out of competitions because you were scared, you'd look like a fool!
- Or insert anything else you can think of here.......

All these dreams, desires, and goals were stillborn. Were discarded before they even had a chance to blossom into the most amazing, incredible events, journeys, or experiences in your life.

We are too quick to give oxygen to why we can't do it, be it or have it. We let our ideas be just ideas, not the driving force. Your dreams are calling you for a reason, and deep down inside there is untapped potential screaming out to be expressed through you! You have amazing gifts and talents that you are leaving alone, leaving to fester inside and never be expressed.

ENOUGH!

ENOUGH with hiding your light.

ENOUGH with feeling like you're inferior.

ENOUGH with trying to fit in or do it the right way.

ENOUGH with not having what you want! Not living the life of YOUR dreams!

Smash Through Your Comfort Zone

So, you're sick and tired of being stuck, unfocused, self-sabotaging, listening to negativity or failing! You've gotten to this point where you have just had enough and you're sick of fear stopping you from progressing. Fear and Faith, both have you believing in the unseen. It's amazing though, how much more time and energy we put into fear instead of faith. Ask yourself, when was the last time you had to do something that stretched you out of your comfort zone?

For example: -

- Talk on stage
- Present something to a group
- Have a difficult conversation
- Start something new
- Stop something that's unhealthy for you
- Start a relationship
- Start a job
- Start a business
- Quit a job

- Quit a relationship
- Meet new people
- Start a new sport or hobby
- Learn a new skill
- Move towns

When faced with stretching outside of your comfort zone, did you automatically make a mental list of all the awesome things that will happen to you? Or did you automatically worry about everything that could possibly go wrong? Does your dominant feeling go to fear or faith?

I have a feeling you went straight to the negative, to fear instead of faith! That's totally normal, that's just you stretching outside of your comfort zone. And every time we do this, we hit up against what is known as our Terror Barrier! The Terror Barrier is an important tool I learned from Bob Proctor. There are a set of steps before you smash through the fear and annihilate your Terror Barrier. Once you've smashed through the Terror Barrier, there is always freedom on the other side!

So, let's learn about the four stages of the Terror Barrier and how to never let fear or your comfort zone stop you ever again!

The first stage is where you notice that you want to change. It's when you are sick of being sick and tired and you decide you want something different. This stage is simply where you plant the idea of what it is you want in your conscious mind. Just like planting a seed, you will plant the idea of a new goal or dream in your conscious mind.

The second stage is where you nurture the positive thoughts and feelings you've started to plant in your conscious mind, and they are taking hold in your subconscious mind. You start getting even more emotionally attached to the new goal, dream, or desire and you start affirming that repetitiously over and over. This new way of being hasn't properly stuck just yet, but you are feeling more and more like this is the new way of being. This stage can be very uncomfortable because it's the stage where you're in the in-between! You're still doing actions that support old results, but you're nurturing the new idea of what it is you want. This part is the push and pull, it can be very uncomfortable during this stage. This is where a lot of people want to give up. It's all too hard and they are wanting to throw in the towel. This is where you NEED to have faith, pay no attention to outside circumstances, and push through. This is where you are HITTING up against the Terror Barrier and it's REALLY Uncomfortable.

Faith and Fear both require you to believe in the unseen. Neither of them is real, so the choice is yours.

From here, the new way of being, the new goal, idea, dream, or desire, is starting to take over in your subconscious mind, the part of the mind that is the control centre. You're feeling more and more like this is your new normal, but the old way of being still has strong roots. It just takes that next step, that next action, that next push to break through into the Terror Barrier. Most people here, will just give up, give in, and bounce right back to their starting point. If you keep bouncing off the

Terror Barrier, you'll always go back to the first stage of the process and start all over again.

How do you break through the Terror Barrier? Great question! You already have all the tools and strategies inside you to break through your Terror Barrier. You wouldn't have this Terror Barrier if you weren't also able to break through into freedom. It all goes down to where you put your energy and actions.

Fear and faith are both unseen, however, have huge control over our energy. When we bounce off the Terror Barrier and go back to the first stage, feeling frustrated, that's us giving in to our fears. When we smash through the Terror Barrier and experience freedom, we are stepping into faith. It's all about the actions we choose to take. Here are some suggested actions you can take to smash through the Terror Barrier:

- Have a detailed plan for your goal
- Follow your strategies to achieve your goal
- Focus on the process
- Set up a Rockstar Attitude
- Use affirmations to affirm your desires and goals: Everything is working out for me.
- Make a list of Goal Achieving Actions and do one per day

You have so got this. Don't let the Terror Barrier ever stop you again from achieving what you want!

Proving My Grandfather Wrong

I had always wanted to be a teacher. I was ten when I knew I loved teaching and I loved children (so funny, because I was a child myself). I was that child that would entertain other people's kids at parties or offer to babysit cousins on the school holidays. I just knew I was meant to be a teacher.

All throughout my schooling, I had a self-image that I wasn't very smart, so I was worried I wouldn't make the grades to get into University to study teaching. That's when I decided I wanted to be a governess instead. A governess is someone who lives on remote properties and teaches the children that live there, through Distance Education, a remote learning system. The governess was like a teacher, but you didn't have to be qualified, you were more like a teacher's aide, helping the children on the property through their schoolwork under the guidance of the Distance Education Teacher.

On Christmas day, when I was fifteen years old, my grandfather asked me what I wanted to do with myself once I'd left school. I said to him that I wanted to be a Governess. To his disgust, he scoffed and informed me, that I should just leave School now if that's all I wanted to do.

I was shocked, annoyed, and determined to show him. So, I up-leveled my goal and instead of being a governess, I decided to pursue my original dream of becoming a Primary school teacher. I'd show him that I did deserve to be educated and my dreams were important.

This new wave of bravery felt very foreign and scary. I didn't know how I was going to get into University to study teaching and how I was then going to be confident enough to stand in front of a classroom of 30 children all looking at me.

My Grandfather's comments were the catalyst for me to stretch outside of my comfort zone. I had to now apply myself to my studies, focus on my goal and start believing in myself. It could have been easy for me to give in to my limiting beliefs, but I knew I wanted to achieve this dream. For the next two years of my schooling, my grades gradually improved, and I knew what I needed to accomplish to be able to attend Uni.

I remember filling out my University preference on the newly installed computers at my school. With my fingers crossed, I completed the forms as to what I wanted to study and which University I wanted to attend. I would then have to wait six weeks until the results would be shared. The following weeks felt like years! This was going to determine if my hard work had paid off or not.

The time finally came when our High School graduation results were released and if I'd been successful in my endeavours. Much to my delight and relief, I easily got the grades to become a Primary School Teacher and was so excited to know that I'd achieved a big goal that I was so proud of.

When I graduated from University with a Bachelor of Education, I was only the second person in my extended family to have a University degree (following my older sister Gaye who studied accounting). During my teaching career, I taught in Schools all throughout Central and Western Queensland enjoying the rural-based schools in the middle of nowhere the most. I even travelled to England (like every other Aussie) and taught in Schools based in Southeast London. This was a great experience but give me country kids any day!

CHAPTER 8

What If It Could Be Easy?

In this chapter, I'll introduce you to my very sexy, very easy formula that I teach my clients when it comes to everything in life! This chapter might go against your limiting beliefs, so take notice of how you feel when reading it. Enjoy!

I'm sure that people on properties have lots of children so they have lots of helping hands! That's what I thought as a kid, anyway. So, my parents have 4 children and as soon as we could balance (or when we became too annoying for our Mum), we were put on the back of a horse and sent out mustering for the day. I was 3 when I started riding and 4 when I was mustering, being led behind Dad on his horse as we'd muster the cattle and walk them to the yards. It was always an adventure, climbing up onto my big horse Jay, who was a tall bay mare, very quiet and had the most beautiful nature. From the back of Jay I could see everything. Although I was a long way up, I always felt safe on Jay.

As I grew up, Dad started looking for ways to work smarter especially when mustering and moving cattle. As each child grew up we'd be sent to school and only able to help muster on the weekends or during the school holidays. Then, when we became high school age, not having any high schools close by, we were sent to boarding school and mostly only came home on school holidays. I remember most school holidays were spent mustering, doing cattle work, or helping on the property. As my birthday would always fall on the September school holidays, we were always doing cattle work in the morning, birthday cake for morning tea and back into the yards for the rest of the day. When I was ten years old, Dad decided to buy a working dog. He bought this beautiful long-haired border collier called Traveller. Traveller was a smart dog with great cattle sense and natural ability. Traveller was trained before coming to us, so knew what to do with the cattle without too much direction from Dad who was only just learning how to train dogs to work cattle.

Traveller would go around the stock easily and effortlessly, bringing back any cattle that strayed, keeping the tale end up and never leaving any cattle behind. He'd find cattle that were hiding in scrub or trying to take off in the opposite direction. Traveller would run and run, tongue out, but never tiering, no matter how far we'd go, he always seemed to have endless amounts of energy. As long as there was a trough to jump in and quench his thirst, he would refresh and keep on going.

One day while mustering, I was about 12 years old, and we were rounding up cattle in a paddock to bring together and walk to the cattle yards to draft. Well, I was cantering along because I could see cattle off in the distance and suddenly, I could hear this loud yelling coming from my Dad. I look over and he's yelling and waving his arm around, signalling to come back. I could even hear him swearing as his command was not being addressed. I couldn't fully understand exactly what he was saying but could definitely hear the odd swear word clearly sailing on the wind as it made its way to me. I thought Dad must have been yelling and swearing at the dog, Traveller, because he was running beside my horse. He would never be swearing at one of his children like this, would he? But, as the yelling became much clearer, I realised Dad was not directing his cursing at the dog...It was actually me, he was yelling, swearing, and telling me to get out of the way of the dog! Yes, it was very clear, what the pecking order was in the paddock!

Traveller was more than just an awesome dog. He replaced a person or two when it came to mustering. By having him there, he was able to get in so many places, keep the cattle going and move so quickly, that you could even muster solo when you had Traveller as your sidekick! Having a working dog meant that Dad could move cattle by himself easily, or one of us kids could take Traveller on the 4-wheeler and put the milker or sheep in the pen overnight. Because Traveller was such a great help, Dad started to buy and breed more cattle dogs to help on the property. These dogs were so great that they would replace manpower when mustering or moving cattle from paddock to paddock. They were also great companions when doing the water run or having to fix fences. I never felt lonely when there were dogs around and each dog had its own unique traits and personality. They really were extensions of the family, however, were never allowed inside the house or even up on the veranda. They were very low-fuss animals but extremely intelligent, friendly, and loyal.

What I did love about this dog, is no matter how big the job, how large the bull, or how angry the cow, Traveller was always there making it look effortless and easy. He was bread for this exact job. He was in his genius zone, doing what he loved and living on a pat, a handful of dog biscuits and a good run to stay happy and going. I learnt so much from that dog Traveller and he still holds a beautiful space in my heart.

Traveller was happy to run beside the bike, go out mustering and round up cattle, have his dog biscuits and sleep in his log. He lived a full life for a working dog and was rewarded with loads of pats, cuddles, and words of praise. This really got me thinking about what we do as people. We want to complicate things, make them difficult, and make it hard for ourselves. The phrase that comes to mind is No Pain, No Gain! What if we could keep it simple, like Traveller? Recognize our gifts and talents, excel in our genius zone, and make a huge impact in our community or even the world.

Are You Making A Mountain Out of A Molehill?

It's a human trait to quickly jump to the worst-case scenario when it comes to achieving our goals! We will have an idea, a light bulb, a deep burning desire, a fantastic hairy scary goal and in the VERY next second, our thoughts will turn to why we can't do it, how we don't deserve what we want, or we're not good enough to have it all. This is as natural to us as breathing oxygen! And unfortunately for some people, it's their default setting! We will automatically jump to the feelings we don't want:

- Overthinking
- Stress
- Fear
- Worry
- Doubt
- Negativity

But the worst thing we do when going after our goals and dreams is to overcomplicate things.

We have been conditioned to think we either don't deserve the things we want, or it's difficult to receive the things we want.

As a child your subconscious mind is completely open, taking in all of your surrounding environment. Your conscious mind doesn't fully develop until you're about seven or eight years of age when you start having an internal dialogue. Therefore, in the years before you turn seven, you are like a sponge, absorbing everything!

So, if you were from a family environment that was supportive and uplifting, then you will most likely have a healthy image of yourself and your abilities. However, if you were surrounded by people who were negative either towards themselves or others and would always criticise ridicule, or blame, then your self-image may not be as positive as you'd like. This might be the time where you think I'm now blaming your parents or primary caregivers for your sh*tty results. But, believe me, I'm not. They did the best job they could do with the information and knowledge they had. And I'm also not excusing those actions that were abusive or violent. This is just my way of explaining in an easy-to-understand terms so that if my 5-year-old son, or my 95-year-old grandfather, were to read this book, they too could both understand it and make huge transformations in their lives!

When you were born, your mind was a blank slate, and whatever your family of origin, your community, your culture and even the media you consumed, helped to shape, and mould the person you have become today. As children, we are bombarded by lots and lots of information and because our subconscious minds are completely open and accepting of everything before the age of seven, we absorb all that is seen, felt, or heard. It all goes into your subconscious mind. And from there, you've decided that it must be a fact. This must be the truth of who you really are! However, unconsciously to ourselves this isn't the truth of who we are. This is just a collection of beliefs, behaviours, and paradigms from those around us, that's kept us safe, protected, alive and experiencing some level of success. There's also probably a pretty healthy dose of not feeling good enough, self-loathing or perfectionism that also goes with this. That's how we know it's NOT the real you. You are born perfect, with a clean slate! You are all-knowing, all-loving and vibrating at such a high frequency because you're not carrying any baggage from your past. That's why people want to get close to newborn babies and you'll hear people say, 'I just want to eat you all up!' They are vibrating at such a high frequency; they don't have any limiting beliefs or paradigms hindering them from living in the present moment.

The negative beliefs and paradigms we have of ourselves, then become your belief systems and influence our behaviour and actions. And most of the time, we are doing the things we do without knowing where they have come from, we are doing them unconsciously. Unknowing to ourselves why we do the things we do and get the results we get, even if we don't want those results anymore.

So, if you were told enough times as a kid that you were never on time, weren't neat enough, weren't smart enough, should be seen and not heard. You'll start creating a belief or paradigm about yourself that supports what you were predominantly told or believed about yourself. How did you learn to walk? You learnt through repetition. How did you learn who you are? You learnt through repetition. However, just because you have a blueprint of genetic material from your parents and grew up in an environment that supports the limiting beliefs you now have, doesn't mean this is your destiny. You have the power to change and create whatever you want for your future!

KISS

KISS! You know what it usually stands for: Keep It Simple Stupid. Well, about 12 years ago, I realised that there were words that had a heavy meaning. And these words were known as shaming words. People would use them, especially with children to keep them under control or their excitement and energy in check. These words were used as a way of being both funny and pointed or at times, not even funny, just cruel. Shaming words are demeaning, put people down and are just not words I personally use or allow my children to use.

Examples of these words and phrases using shaming words are:

- Silly
- Stupid
- Idiot
- Dumb
- Dummy
- D*ckhead

- Ding dong
- Dope
- I'm just being silly
- I always overact
- I'm such a fool
- I always make a fool of myself

So, when I would say KISS- Keep It Simple Stupid, it just never really rang true with me. I felt uncomfortable saying the word stupid. I also hated hearing other people say any of those shaming words or phrases about themselves or others. When someone would say how silly they had been. I would quickly jump in and reply with 'Don't you talk about my friend like that.' I hated hearing anyone talk like this, it just makes me feel a bit sad, because if they knew the potential, they have just underneath the surface, the magnificence that radiates from within. Then they would never say those things about themselves or anyone else ever again. It's as if they are beating up on, putting down or scolding the child within. It just hasn't and never will feel right to me. That's when I decided I had to change the word 'Stupid' to 'SEXY'. Yes, that's right, there's a little bit (or a lot) of sexy in all of us. So, I soon coined the phrase- Keep It Simple Sexy and I love using this when talking about keeping everything super simple, easy, and fun. I also love saying Keep It Simple Sexy and watch people's faces light up, go bright red, or give a cheeky giggle. It's so much fun shifting those old limiting paradigms and replacing them with super fun, empowering or cheeky ones!

This journey of getting to know and understand us better, shouldn't be difficult or hard. At times it might feel uncomfortable, annoying, frustrating, too long, or any other word you want to put in there. But it doesn't have to be! It can be an easy, fun, simple process that you can decide to do right here, right now and have HUGE impact in your life.

I love contradicting the old paradigms that say:

- No pain no gain
- Got to work hard
- If you didn't work hard, it's not worth it
- Nothing good comes easy or free
- Only the wicked get things easily!

So, I decided enough is enough and we need to make this an easy process that can be understood if you're 5 or 95 years of age! So, I wanted to make this a simple, easy process, a KISS process so that all the people I love in my life can implement and have a huge impact in their life as soon as possible!

Whenever you get the urge to make things difficult, or complicated or start overthinking, stressing, and allowing your anxiety to rise…remember, we are going to Keep It Simple Sexy and often the easiest answer, the pathway of least resistance is the pathway we need to take!

Pathway of least resistance, let me share a little bit about this. Because we are human and our default is to make things difficult, we usually overlook the most obvious way. We think there must be a catch, this is too easy, how can this be? Neville Goddard talks about how the Universe is always providing the pathway of least resistance. It's us, as humans who make it difficult. I want you to think of a time that you have wanted something, and it came too easily. Or, if you were thinking of someone and they happened to ring you. I've noticed many clients who say yes to the coaching, and before they know it, they receive money to pay the deposit, or a grandmother sends them money to pay for the coaching. It was so super easy. This is the pathway of least resistance. There is one super important key ingredient in the pathway of least resistance... it's this key area called- Decision.

Making a decision is the key ingredient you need when applying the KISS formula. All you need to do is to decide what you want. Those who make decisions quickly and are unshakable in their belief are the winners. Once a decision is made, all the people, place, resources and money, falls into place and everything you wanted arrives. Again, this is really simple, we are the ones who want to overcomplicate things. We are the ones who second guess, overthink and talk ourselves out of the decisions we make.

We know that we could have more, do more, and be more, and yet, we keep blocking ourselves, self-sabotaging and even getting in our own way! However, the past is in the past and your journey here was all meant to be! You're here reading this book right now because you are doing exactly what you're meant to be doing and these words are specifically meant for YOU.

To KISS your goals, your dreams, or your desires, all you need to do is make a decision. Decide that you want this, you deserve this and you're going to go after this with everything you've got. KISS is all about looking for the pathway of least resistance and enjoying the amazing things that have always been waiting for you. This is your time, are you ready to really jump amongst all the goodness, all the glory and all the prosperity you deserve? This is your life! Why not live it to the fullest, you sexy thing?

Emma's Story

Emma desperately wanted to work with me, but she didn't have the money for the coaching deposit. So, I told her about my KISS formula to manifest anything you want! I'm all about Keep It Simple Sexy and when I talked to Emma about getting the coaching deposit, I said, let's keep this really simple and easy.

My KISS Manifesting Formula goes like this: Ask, Believe, Receive. You can access this in digital form at www.gerryhuston.com.au

Now, you look at the formula and you think it's too simple, there's got to be a catch, or it's got to be harder than that! But, nope, there it is, as simple as Ask, Believe, Receive.

Ask for what you want. Be really clear on what it is you want. If you're not being clear, then you're putting mixed messages out into the Universe and you'll receive bits and pieces of what you want, but not the whole thing. Being crystal clear in what you want, is the first step in KISS manifesting.

Believe you can have what you want. Believe it on a deep level an unwavering, unshakable belief. Just as you know the sun will come up tomorrow and set in the evening, this is the same belief you need for the KISS manifesting formula. Believe to the core of your being, that this is for you, and it will show up in the physical world.

And finally, sit back and wait to receive what it is you want. This step most people find the most difficult part because you are allowing it to happen, not forcing it. A lot of people want to force their manifestations and the lack of control is frustrating! Allow your manifestation to appear in the physical world by letting go. Imagine you're in a relationship and your partner is being over-controlling, possessive and obsessive about you. It's not sexy, it's really unattractive and ends up pushing the other person away. The same thing can be said for our manifestations and goals. Don't be the obsessive paranoid partner, set and forget your manifestation, allowing it to come to you when it's ready.

It is that simple! Ask, Believe, Receive. I teach all my coaching clients this simple formula and I have so many questions and queries as to why this shouldn't and couldn't possibly work! However, it works every time.

So, Emma went away armed with the KISS Manifestation Formal and she asked for what she wanted. She wanted to manifest $10,000. She wanted this money to pay her deposit for the coaching and fix her car. Emma had no idea where this money was coming from, but that wasn't her worry. That would be taken care of by the pathway of least resistance. All she had to do was Ask, Believe, and Receive. Emma went into this process believing. She believed that she could receive this money and that it was going to be easy.

The very next day, her beautiful Grandmother came to visit her. Her Grandmother said to Emma, that she wanted to give her Granddaughter a gift. And as she was saying this, her Grandmother handed her a cheque that was made out to her for $10,000. Now, my client was ecstatic, but she was also questioning whether the Universe was testing her, so she declined the money. My client had asked for what she wanted, believed it could happen, and then finally receive it, but declined! So, when I was talking to her 24 hours later, I asked her how she was going. She mentioned what had happened and said that she refused to take the cheque from her Grandmother. I asked her why and she said that the Universe must have just been testing her. I said to her that the Universe always picks the pathway of least resistance! So, this was the receiving part of the manifesting formula and all she had to do was receive it. Emma went back to her Grandmother to graciously accept her generous offer, only to find that her Grandmother had misplaced the cheque and couldn't find it anymore.

Emma then decided to do the Ask, Believe, Receive formula again. Two days later her Grandmother called her and informed her that she had found the cheque and Emma this time, graciously received and celebrated her magnificent power.

Don't overcomplicate things! The best thing you can do is trust yourself and believe in KISS- Keep It Simple Sexy!

CHAPTER 9

Teamwork Makes the Dream Work

Everything works together in some way or another. This chapter will highlight the importance of teamwork and how your goals will inspire others around you. You never know who's watching your journey!

I think we all get to a point as a teenager where we get sick of our parents, it's very normal to feel like this, I'm sure I wasn't alone! I was at the ripe old age of thirteen and I was sick of them! The main reason I was over my parents, was because they were making me do jobs (how dare they)! Every afternoon, there were three core jobs that had to be done. Feeding the chooks, feeding, locking up the dogs, and emptying the rubbish. It was usually rotated between my siblings and I, one week you were on chooks, the next you were on dogs, and the following week you were on rubbish and then the cycle started up again.

Look, it doesn't really sound like much now, but at thirteen, I thought it was really inconvenient having to do a ten-minute job every afternoon. I've since found that adulting is tough and a ten-minute job was really nothing! But, as a teenager, it felt totally unfair!

I got to a point where I had decided enough was enough and I informed my parents that it was very unfair that I had to do afternoon jobs! considering I had a ninety-minute bus trip one way to school, a whole day of learning, only to come home and painfully complete my homework to then be expected to help around the house also. I shared my displeasure with my parents about this inequity and I'm sure it went against child labour laws!

What conspired next, is one of the most important lessons I've learned. My very loving and patient parents shared with me something I now use with my own children.

My parents calmly sat me down at the table on the back veranda. Having not really voiced my opinion like this in the past, I thought for sure I'd be in so much trouble! My family wasn't above smacking, and I thought I was definitely in for a smack for sure. However, they sat me down and said they wanted to have a chat with me. This was uncharted water, having a chat must have meant I was REALLY in trouble! However, I will never forget that conversation and the learnings from it, I use to this very day.

They sat me down and asked me to share my grievances about doing jobs. Why I didn't want to continue with this role and why I thought it was so unfair to be expected to do jobs! My parents said to me; 'For anything to work on this property and in our family, we need to all work together. You are a very important part of this team and what you do is important and keeps the whole team going.' They highlighted to me that I was an important part of the family, like how the egg is an integral ingredient in a cake. Without the egg in the cake mixture, the mixture doesn't bind together as well, and you might end up with a runny or crumbly cake. Therefore, even if you think you're insignificant, don't hold a big role or you also hate feeding the chooks, before you give up, remember that you're also an integral part of the whole process in your family, your company, your career, your community, your business, your relationships.

Teamwork, Makes the Dream Work!

What's the Point?

I work with a lot of women who have lost their mojo, their purpose, the reason they spring out of bed each and every morning with excitement, not because the kids are up at the crack of dawn again! These women come to me because they know they want more, but they just don't know how or even where to start.

On the outside, these women appear to have it all.

They have:

- A great husband
- Wonderful kids
- A career or business they love
- A social life that's active
- And they try and stay fit

But these women still feel like there is something missing. Like there's a hole, an empty space, aching to be filled with their passion, their purpose, giving back, showing up, or shining the light from within. So many women are sleepwalking through their life. It's like Groundhog Day, the same thing repeated day after day after day. They feel like they're on the treadmill of life, no matter how fast they run, they don't seem to get any further forward. They put everyone else's needs before their own. Their kids, their husband, their extended family, their community, and their work all comes before themselves. When the end of the day rolls around, they just don't have the energy, mental space, or capacity to do anything for themselves, let alone even think about what drives them, energises them, or spurs them along. They are stuck, blocked and shadows of their former outgoing, bubbly, strong confident selves.

You might think, 'What do these women have to complain about!' And yes, you might have a point. But also, why is it ok that these women, who have so much to give, contribute, and offer, also have a full and exciting existence, just fade away into the background?

It's not good enough that it's ok for women to feel unfulfilled like they don't matter, and their voices shouldn't be heard. There is so much untapped potential that lies just underneath the surface, and we aren't even tapping into this! We could be able to have anything we want, be anything we want, and experience anything we want at whatever age we are.

Life should only get better and better every year! Our dreams grow sweeter, and our goals become more ambitious! However, our energy is being pulled and our focus is becoming scattered. It feels like we have so much more in our life now to make them easier, but we have less time, less clarity, and less

The real travesty here is that these women feel they don't know how to find their mojo, their purpose and how to share that with the world. All that untapped potential is going to die when they do. All the amazing stories, ideas, creations, thoughts, products, services, gifts, and opportunities that lay just beneath the surface, will disappear forever. Life doesn't stop when you're out of your 30s, life has only just really begun. It's living for yourself and what you want.

Why not complain about not having your mojo, not living your purpose, the reason you were put here on earth? It might not appear to be a travesty to some, but this is your life and you're only here for a limited time, why not live a large, beautiful, exciting, life of purpose? A life that lights you up, gets you excited, and makes you want to show up as your authentic self and do what it is that you're meant to do...whatever that looks like.

It's your time to shine.

What if Your Dream Isn't Even About You?

What if the solution to you having everything you want, isn't even about you?

I remember when I had my first child, and my Grandmother came to see him at the hospital. My Grandmother loved babies, loved children, and even before I was married, suggested I have an accident (meaning fall pregnant out of wedlock) because she really wanted a Great-Grandchild to cuddle. Even bought me a sexy nighty for Christmas that year, in case she had been too subtle with her audible suggestion.

So, when my Grandmother came to visit me at the hospital to meet my newborn son, I was still at that stage where I was overly protective and so tired, I could hardly keep my eyes open from the exhaustion of giving birth, learning how to breastfeed and being woken up all hours of the night and day by this tiny alarm clock that needed feeding. As my Grandmother was cuddling my newborn son, looking down at his beautiful fresh squishy face. She said to me, 'Now Geraldine, you know that children are for everyone.' I didn't know this. This was news to me! This was in fact the first time I had ever heard this. And I pressed her with what she meant by this. She said 'Children are such a gift that brings so much love and joy into your world. Children are to be shared, cuddled by many, and raised by a village.' I was so moved by what she said. Here I thought my husband and I were on our own to raise this little pink, squishy, beautiful baby boy. But here my Grandmother was telling me, that it takes more than just a family to raise a child, it takes a village. And together we support, nurture, and love each other to create strong resilient communities.

This mindset allowed me to feel more comfortable when asking for help with my children from friends and family. It encouraged me to build a community for other parents who didn't have the luxury of their family being close and helping them out where possible. It also gave me the confidence to hand my then five-month-old baby, to an elderly lady who looked sad and desperate for a cuddle, while we travelled on a tram in Melbourne.

What if you stepped into your power, your gifts, your wealth your dreams weren't even actually for you but to support, encourage and be the example for those around you?

What if it was for those watching you, going along with you on the journey? Your friends, your family, your loved ones. What if by you forging the path, you were giving permission to others to do the same for themselves in their life?

By you living your most abundant, healthiest, wealthiest, happiest, most joyful life, those around you are also given permission to do the same thing.

It's not about you, means that it's about those watching you. Who is watching you? Watching every step you take, every triumph you have, every tough time you've dragged yourself back up again? Who's watching you that you don't even know?

Is it:

- Your children
- Your family
- Your community
- Your niece
- Your colleagues
- Your enemies
- Your next-door neighbours
- People in other countries
- People in all different states of Australia
- Other regional or rural women
- Businesswomen

- That little girl who's desperately looking for someone who reflects herself.
- People living in totally different countries to you

Or is the most important person in your world watching you, taking everything in that you do, listening to everything you say and think? Are you watching you?

Much like my Grandmother said to me, children are for everyone. Maybe our goals are for everyone's benefit, not just our own. To find out more about this go to www.gerryhuston.com.au

How does you achieving your goals benefit others? This might be a strange question because we usually set and achieve our goals because WE want it, not necessarily because we think it will impact others in a positive way. I want you to start thinking of your goals and how it benefits everyone! How will achieving my goal benefit yourself? How will achieving my goal benefit my family or community? And how would you achieving your goal benefit the world?

I want you to write a list of all the benefits of you achieving your goal, bring to you:

- I will be more wealthy
- I will be fit, hot, and sexy
- I will feel happier

Now, ask yourself; How does me achieving my goal benefit those people directly in your life, your family, your partner, your kids, and your neighbours:

- Take my kids on a holiday
- Buy a bigger house for us all to live in
- Contribute to the household income
- Live a longer and healthier life with my kids
- Be more present with my loved ones

Finally, ask yourself: How does me achieving my goal benefit the wider community, your nation, or even positively impact the world:

- I am an example for others on a global scale
- The ripple effect of circulating more money within my local community
- Increase in jobs both locally and globally
- I give permission for others to step into their power, and potential and create the life they love

Far too many times, we cap ourselves in what we think we can do, be or have. But what if your success wasn't even about you? It was about those who you can impact on a local, national or global basis. What if your goal was bigger than you and you didn't really need it, after all, it was always about showing up for others, pathing the way, and being the inspirational role model, you were always born to be. About being heard, being important, being listened to!

Not only do you benefit when you achieve a goal. Your wealth increases, your health gets better, and you're living a more authentic happy life. You create a community a team a following. And together teamwork makes the dream work.

Jill's Story

I want to share with you a story about one of my favourite clients, named Jill who lives in outback Central Queensland on a beautiful cattle property. The property is a well-established prosperous enterprise and has been for many years. Jill is married to a supportive and loving husband, who is also her co-owner and partner in both business and life. Jill's three children are all grown now and starting to have families of their own. This makes Jill very happy and excited that she has now become a Grandmother and enjoys all of the fun parts this new role brings.

Looking from the outside in, you'd think that Jill has it all together. She has a great relationship, a well-established business, independent grown children, and gorgeous Grandchildren. However, Jill was not feeling like her life was fulfilling her. She had given her years to home-schooling her children, supporting them through adolescence and through marriages, and now into having children of their own. The property was her husband's passion and he lived for the land. He loved every aspect of property life and work, and this was more than a business for him, it was a way of life, a lifestyle that he has wanted to be involved in since birth. Jill had also given years to her local community which she loved dearly and was so proud to be a part of.

Jill, loved her family, love the business she had helped establish with her husband, but she still felt like there was something still missing. And she knew she wanted to be a little bit more positive, a little bit happier, and wanted to live a life that was a little bit bigger. Jill knew there were adventures she wanted to have, things she wanted to acquire, experiences she wanted to endure, and people she wanted to inspire. But she was also unsure of how to achieve these things.

When everything looks so great from the outside, it's really difficult to not be satisfied with your life. It feels almost selfish to want more. She should just be happy with what she's got and that should be it. Don't get me wrong, Jill was a very successful person and when she put her mind towards what she wanted, she got it! But what she also noticed, is that it only lasted for short amounts of time.

Jill knew that this wasn't an existence that she wanted to have. She didn't want to just be satisfied with what she's got and get on with the rest of her life. She wanted to feel amazing about her life, feel like her life mattered and she was making a difference. Jill wanted to not only survive the rest of her life, but she wanted to THRIVE! As she knew all too well, life is short, and you've really got to make the most of every day!

Jill took the leap to become a coaching client and hasn't looked back since. Jill decided that her goals and dreams were important, and they were important enough to go after them with everything she's got.

Jill was excited about starting this journey because she knew that this was what she was looking for. Jill wanted a formula to achieve her goals, even the big ones. But she didn't want to do it the hard way. She had spent so many of her years doing the hard slog, doing things the hard way, and living by the motto of 'No pain, no gain'! This was not what Jill wanted to continue for the rest of her life. She wanted to be able to achieve things in an easier, calmer, and more focused way. Jill was ready to make a quantum leap with her results!

As Jill learned the formula to create the life and business of her dreams, things started to transform for her. Jill started to let go of the old limiting beliefs she had carried for decades and started thinking in a more positive way.

Jill noticed that the things that would have upset her in the past, or made her mad, really didn't affect her at all now. She went through life relaxed, peaceful, focused, and calm. Instead of reacting to any problem that arise, Jill responded in a calm and confident manner, knowing that there will always be an outcome that benefited all involved. It wasn't only Jill's personal life that was improving, things were improving in the day-to-day running of the business too.

You might be scared about taking the leap, and you might worry about investing time and money into yourself. But, what if it's not about you, it's about those around you? It's not about what you can have, you can get, buy, or acquire. What if it's about who you inspire, who you motivate, and who you give permission to for others to start turning up in their life in a big way?

I have no doubt that Jill will now achieve everything she's ever wanted and MORE. Now Jill has the tools, strategies, and desire to push herself further. Go deeper than she has before and show up in the most magnificent way!

I'm excited about all the people Jill has now inspired by her story, just by Jill deciding that something had to change and acting on that feeling. Each and every one of us has more to give, more to gain, and more to learn about ourselves. By hearing Jill's story I know this will inspire many people to not only be grateful for where they currently are but for them to also stretch, grow and live a purpose-filled life.

Author

Gerry Huston is a Mum, Author, and Public Speaker, who is also known as The Rural Mindset Coach. From cowboy boots to heels, Gerry has had a variety of vocations, such as being a jillaroo, mining camp cleaner, Primary School Teacher, NLP Practitioner, and now Life Coach.

Gerry Huston has experienced firsthand the isolation felt by businesswomen living in regional areas. For the past 11 years, she has worked with hundreds of women globally who were geographically isolated or felt alone in their business. This is the driver behind her passion for providing high-quality coaching and resources to women in remote communities, helping them transform their businesses and lives.

When she isn't coaching or creating, Gerry can be found in the middle of nowhere, toasting marshmallows over an open fire with her husband, Tim, and their two energetic boys.

www.ingramcontent.com/pod-product-compliance
Lightning Source LLC
Chambersburg PA
CBHW070306010526
44107CB00056B/2502